Teach Yourself Hindi

Mohini Rao

HIPPOCRENE BOOKS
New York

First Hippocrene Edition, 1990

For information, address: Hippocrene Books, Inc.,
171 Madison Avenue, New York, NY 10016

ISBN 0-87052-831-9 (pbk.)

Printed in the United States by Hippocrene Books, Inc.

FOREWORD

There are several books on the subject of learning Hindi without a guide or a teacher. All that one can learn of a language from reading a book are the basic rules of grammar and a minimal vocabulary, phrases and sentences for everyday use.

The basic vocabulary needed by a person may vary according to his interest or occupation. I have tried to give in this book phrases and sentences used commonly. A minimal dictionary has also been added at the end. Rules of grammar have been explained only where absolutely necessary, for I believe that hearing a language constantly an attentively is the best way of learning it.

Knowledge of fundamental grammatical rules is of course necessary, but more important is to speak the language without inhibition. Mistakes will occur but they will get corrected in the process.

Hearing is important to help you correct your pronunciation and enunciation of words and phrases. A book, even the best one, can help only in a limited way if the language is not heard regularly.

Hindi is a phonetic language. It is written as it is spoken. Unlike English, there is no need to learn spellings. The reader is advised to learn the script from the beginning as it shortens the process of learning and also ensures correct pronunciation. There are some sounds in Hindi which cannot be reproduced accurately in the Roman script.

This book teaches you the spoken Hindi, popularly known as Hindustani which is a pleasant mixture of Hindi and Urdu words understood by all. The key to the pronunciation and the phonetic symbols should be followed as accurately as possible.

In the end I would like to add that the method adopted in this book is based on my own vast personal experience of teaching Hindi to foreigners, and it is an attempt only to teach the rudiments of the language.

I should be happy if this little book benefits foreigners and Indians who wish to learn Hindi the easy way.

New Delhi *Mohini Rao*

CONTENTS

CHAPTER ONE

KEY TO PRONUNCIATION

Phonetic symbols

—This sign over a letter stands for a long *āā* sound. For example,

ā would be pronounced as aa.

would be pronounced as ee.

Mark the difference between a and *ā*, i and , u and *ū*.

Pronounce it loudly many times to get the desired result.

~ This symbol over a letter denotes nasalized sound. For example, *ñ* would be pronounced as *n* with a nasal sound and not as a separate consonant.

• A dot under a letter denotes the hard and aspirated form of a particular consonant. For example,

d (soft dental sound) as in *dāl* (lentils)
ḍ (hard cerebral sound as in *ḍar* (fear)

dh (soft aspirated form as in *dūdh* (milk)
dh (hard aspirated form as in *ḍholăk* (drum)

Vowels

There are twelve vowels in Hindi.

अ	*a*	as in *u*ltra
आ	*ā*	as in f*a*ther
इ	*i*	as in *i*nk, p*i*nk
ई	*ī*	as in f*ee*l, n*ee*d
उ	*u*	as in p*u*ll, b*u*ll
ऊ	*ū*	as in m*oo*n, t*oo*l
ए	*ē*	as in r*a*y, g*a*y
ऐ	*ai*	as in *a*ngle
ओ	*o*	as in s*o*, *o*ver
औ	*au*	as in c*o*llege
अं	*nga*	as in hu*n*ger
अः	*ah*	as in ah
अ		is also written as अ

Consonants

There are thirty-six consonants.

क	*ka*	as in kite
ख	*kha*	(aspirated *ka*)
ग	*ga*	as in go

घ	*gha*	(aspirated *ga*)
ङ	*nga*	a nasal sound as in stung
च	*cha*	as in chair
छ	*chha*	(aspirated *cha.*)
ज	*ja*	as in jar
झ	*jha*	(aspirated *ja*)
ट	*ṭa*	as in talk
ठ	*ṭha*	(aspirated *ta*)
ड	*ḍa*	as in dog
ढ	*ḍha*	(aspirated *da*)
त	*ta*	this soft dental sound is not in the English language
थ	*tha*	soft aspirated form of *ta*
द	*da*	soft dental sound. Not found in English.
ध	*dha*	(aspirated *da*)
न	*na*	as in nose
प	*pa*	as in pulp
फ	*pha*	(aspirated *pa.*)
ब	*ba*	as in bun
भ	*bha*	(aspirated *ba.*)
म	*ma*	as in mother
य	*ya*	as in yellow

र	*ra*	as in rubber (r is always rolled)
ल	*la*	as in lull
व	*va*	as in verb
श	*sha*	as in shudder
ष	*ṣha*	Since the distinction between श and ष is very subtle, and the sound almost the same, both the letters are represented here by Roman letters *sha*. To mark the distinction in the written form a dot has been added under s in the case of ष. श is a palatal sound and ष is cerebral. The beginners need not worry too much about this as the cerebral ष is not used often.
स	*sa*	as in sulk
ह	*ha*	as in hunger
क्ष	*ksha*	no equivalent sound in English
त्र	*tra*	as in truck with a soft dental *t*.
ज्ञ	*jna*	no equivalent sound in English.

Consonants at a glance

क	ख	ग	घ	ङ
ka	*kha*	*ga*	*gha*	*nga*

च	छ	ज	झ	ञ
cha	*chha*	*ja*	*jha*	*nya*
ट	ठ	ड	ढ	ण
ṭ	*ṭha*	*ḍa*	*ḍha*	*ṇa*
त	थ	द	ध	न
ta	*tha*	*da*	*dha*	*na*
प	फ	ब	भ	म
pa	*pha*	*ba*	*bha*	*ma*
य	र	ल	व	
ya	*ra*	*la*	*va*	
श	ष	स	ह	
sha	*ṣha*	*sa*	*ha*	
क्ष	त्र	ज्ञ		
ksha	*tra*	*jna*		

It would be noticed above that the two sets of consonants त थ द ध and ट ठ ड ढ have been represented by the same set of English consonants *t, tha, da* and *dha*. To mark the difference in the pronunciation the dental consonants त थ द ध have been represented by *ṭa, tha, da* and *dha* and the second set of cerebral consonants have a dot under them, as explained earlier in the paragraph on Phonetic Symbols. For example:

त	*ta*	थ	*tha*	द	*da*	ध	*dha*
ट	*ṭa*	ठ	*ṭha*	ड	*ḍa*	ढ	*ḍha*

It is important to understand this to help not only the correct pronunciation, but to be able to distinguish one sound from another, as two words like *dal* and *ḍal* have entirely different meanings. (*dal* means lentils and *ḍal* a branch of a tree.)

There are two more letters ड़ and its aspirated form ढ़ which are used very often although they do not figure in the *varṇamālā* (alphabet). They will be written in the Roman script here as *ṛ* (ड़) and *ṛh* (ढ़).

F and Z have been adapted into the Hindi alphabet. These sounds are acquired by adding a dot under फ *pha* and ज *ja*. For example:

फ	*pha*	*phal* (fruit)
फ़	*fa*	*fasal* (crop)
ज	*ja*	*jānā* (to go)
ज़	*za*	*zarūr* (certainly)

Aspirated and Unaspirated Consonants

There are aspirated and unaspirated

groups of consonants. The sound differs by the presence or absence of a puff of air after the initial consonant.

unaspirated		**aspirated**	
क	*ka*	ख	*kha*
ग	*ga*	घ	*gha*
च	*cha*	छ	*chha*
ज	*ja*	झ	*jha*
ट	*ṭa*	ठ	*ṭha*
ड	*ḍa*	ढ	*ḍha*
त	*ta*	थ	*tha*
द	*da*	ध	*dha*
प	*pa*	फ	*pha*
ब	*ba*	भ	*bha*

In English most of the consonants are pronounced with aspiration. It is therefore more difficult for English speaking people to pronounce correctly the soft dental or the unaspirated consonants. People speaking Slav or other European languages do not have this problem to that extent.

One of the most effective ways of being sure of pronouncing the aspirated and unaspirated consonant correctly is to hold a paper or a handkerchief in front of your mouth. When an aspirated consonant is pronounced the paper or the handkerchief will shake slightly. It will remain steady when a consonant is not aspirated. It is very important not only to know the difference while pronouncing, **but also to know the difference while hearing.**

The vowel a is inherent in each consonant, and that is why क has been written as *ka*. The a in a consonant is absent only when the consonant is combined with some other vowel or when it forms a conjunct with another consonant, e.g., when *ka* is combined with *ī* it becomes kī.

The last three letters in the alphabet are compound consonants.

क्ष	*ksha*	is	ka+sha
त्र	*tra*	is	ta+ra
ज्ञ	*jna*	is	ja+na

Complete Varnamala (alphabet) at a glance

अ	आ	इ	ई	उ	ऊ	ए	ऐ
a	*ā*	*i*	*ī*	*u*	*ū*	*ē*	*ai*
ओ	औ	अं	अः				
ō	*au*	*ang*	*ah*				

क	ख	ग	घ	ङ	
ka	*kha*	*ga*	*gha*	*nga*	
च	छ	ज	झ	ञ	
cha	*chha*	*ja*	*jha*	*ṇa*	
ट	ठ	ड	ढ	ण	
ṭa	*tḥa*	*ḍā*	*dḥā*	*ṇa*	
त	थ	द	ध	न	
ta	*tha*	*dā*	*dḥā*	*na*	
प	फ	ब	भ	म	
pa	*pha*	*ba*	*bha*	*ma*	
य	र	ल	व	श	
ya	*ra*	*la*	*va*	*sha*	
ष	स	ह	क्ष	त्र	ज्ञ
ṣha	*sa*	*ha*	*ksha*	*tra*	*jna*

Vowel signs or *mātrā*

A vowel is written as a complete letter only when it is used in the beginning of a word. When it occurs in between a word it is combined with a consonant. This may be called the short form of a vowel, or a ***mātrā*** (vowel sign).

A vowel is pronounced alone but a vowel sign is pronounced together with a consonant. Each vowel is represented by a sign or *mātrā* as given below. It is also shown here how it is combined with a vowel in the script.

Vowel		Sign or *mātrā*	as combined with a consonant	example
अ	(*a*)	has no vowel sign as it is inherent in a consonant		
आ	(*ā*)	ा	क+आ=का *ka+ā=kā*	काला *kālā* (black)
इ	(*i*)	ि	क+इ=कि *ka+i=ki*	किताब *kitāb* (book)
ई	(*ī*)	ी	क+ी=की *ka+ī=kī*	कीमा *kīma* (mince meat)
उ	(*u*)	ु	क+उ=कु *ka+u=ku*	कुरता *kurta* (Indian shirt)
ऊ	(*ū*)	ू	क+ऊ=कू *ka+ū=kū*	कूद *kūd* (jump)

ए	(*e*)		क+ए=के	केला *kēlā* (banana)
			ka+*ē*=*kē*	
ऐ	(*ai*)		क+ऐ=कै	कैसा *kaisā* (how)
			ka+*ai*=*kai*	
ओ	(ō)	ो	क+ो=को	कोना *kōnā* (corner)
			ka+ō=*k*ō	
औ	(*au*)	ौ	क+औ=कौ	कौन *kaun* (who)
			ka+*au*=*kau*	
अं	(*ang*)		क+अं=कं	कंघी *kānghī* (comb)
			ka=*nga*=*kang*	

Note: If the nasal sound comes in the end it will be marked by ँ, e.g., kaha*ñ*.

It would be a good exercise to write this out combining the *mātrās* with different consonants.

ख	खा	खि	खी	खु	खू	खे	खै	खो	खौ	खं	ख:
kha	*khā*	*khi*	*khī*	*khu*	*khū*	*khē*	*khai*	*khō*	*khau*	*khañ*	*khah*
ग	गा	गि	गी	गु	गू	गे	गै	गो	गौ	गं	ग:
ga	*gā*	*gi*	*gī*	*gu*	*gū*	*gē*	*gai*	*go*	*gau*	*gañ*	*gah*
घ	घा	घि	घी	घु	घू	घे	घै	घो	घौ	घं	घ:
gha	*ghā*	*ghi*	*ghī*	*ghu*	*ghū*	*ghē*	*ghai*	*ghō*	*ghau*	*ghañ*	*ghah*
च	चा	चि	ची	चु	चू	चे	चै	चो	चौ	चं	च:
cha	*chā*	*chi*	*chī*	*chu*	*chū*	*chē*	*chai*	*chō*	*chau*	*chañ*	*chah*
छ	छा	छि	छी	छु	छू	छे	छै	छो	छौ	छं	छ:
chha	*chhā*	*chhi*	*chhī*	*chhu*	*chhū*	*chhē*	*chhai*	*chhō*	*chhau*	*chhañ*	*chha*
ज	जा	जि	जी	जु	जू	जे	जै .	जो	जौ	जं	ज:
ja	*jā*	*ji*	*jī*	*ju*	*jū*	*jē*	*jai*	*jō*	*jau*	*jañ*	*jah*

And so on. This exercise would be of help particularly to those who are learning to read and write.

Conjunct Consonants

Now you know how a vowel is combined with a consonant.

A number of words in Hindi have two consonants combined. In such a case the first consonant is written incompletely and joined with the second consonant. For example, if two क are combined:

क+क=क्क

Another way of joining two consonants is to add a stroke under the first letter. This may be easier until you have had a good practice in writing.

क+क=क्‌क

But it would be helpful to know the first method also since while reading that is the more likely form of conjuncts you will come across.

Consonants in Hindi are of two types:

(i) those which have a vertical line in the end, and

(ii) those which do not have a vertical line.

The following consonants come under the first type:

क	ख	ग	घ		च	ज	झ	ञ	ण	त	थ
ध	न		प	फ	ब	भ	म	य	ल	व	श
ष	स		क्ष	त्र	ज्ञ						

The second type:

छ ट ठ ड ढ द र ह

When in a conjunct consonant the first letter has a vertical line, all you have to do is to drop the vertical line in the first letter Example:

ग+व=ग्व

च+छ=च्छ

म+व=म्व

ल+ल=ल्ल

क and फ have a vertical line but they have a hook in the end. When combining them with another consonant the hook is left midway so that it may be joined with the second letter.
Example:

क+क=क्क

क+व=क्व

फ+फ=फ्फ

ट, ठ, ड and ढ cannot be combined in either way. They are, therefore, joined to another consonant by adding a stroke under the first letter.

ट+ट=ट्ट

ट+ड=ट्ड

Sometimes these four letters mentioned above are combined like this:

ट+ट=ट्ट
ट+ठ=ट्ठ
ड+ड=ड्ड

But this way of writing is cumbersome and not attractive. It is better, therefore, to add a stroke to the first letter of the conjunct, ट्, ठ्, ड्, etc.

Now a word about joining र to another consonant. Note these different forms.

कर्म *karma* act, action
क्रम *krama* order, sequence
कृपा *kripā* kindness

1. In the first instance, *karma*, *ra* comes before the last letter *ma*, and appears in the form of a hook on the top of the letter which follows it.

2. In the second example, *krama*, *ra* is joined to the first consonant *ka*, and is in the form of a stroke under it.

3. In the third word, *kripa*, *ra* and *i* are joined to *ka*. If *ra* is combined with ι in a conjunct, it is symbolised as added under the consonant to which it is joined.

More examples:

धर्म	*dharma*	religion
सर्प	*sarpa*	snake
कृष्ण	*Krishna*	Krishna
क्रय	*Kraya*	buying
नृप	*nripa*	king

Please also note that the form कृ or नृ etc. are essentially from Sanskrit and used only in Sanskrit words which have been adopted in Hindi. If you were to write a word like British in Hindi the correct way of writing would be ब्रिटिश and not बृटिश

Joining क and त

क and त are joined as क्त. There is a change of style now, but when you see क्त you should know it is *kta* conjunct.

It has been mentioned earlier that every consonant has an *a* in it, but it has purposely been not added at the end of words ending in consonants to avoid mistakes in pronunciation. Sometimes names are pronounced with an ā ending even if there is *a* at the end of the last consonant. There cannot a be better example than the prevalent mispronunciation, even by Indians, of Ashōka. Hotel. It is now commonly pronounced as Ashōkā Hotel. Even those who know it is named after the great Hindu Emperor Ashōka, cannot help pronouncing it as Ashōka, with a long ā sound in the end. This pronunciation has come to stay. Those who pronounce it correctly find themselves in a minority! However, when two consonants occur in between a word, a has been introduced between them so that they are not mistaken as conjunct consonants.

Syntax

In Hindi the syntax is different from that of English. The verb in Hindi is placed always in the end of a sentence, for example:

I go to school will be in Hindi *mai skūl jātā hūñ* (I to school go)

मेरा नाम राम है *mērā nām Rām hai*
My name Ram is

मेरा घर बड़ा है *mērā ghar baṛā hai*
My house big is

The preposition in Hindi is actually postposition. For example, in English it is said *the book is on the table.* In Hindi it would be *kitāb mēz par hai* (book table on is). पर *par* (on) is placed after *mēz* (table) not before.

Similarly, *gilās mēn pānī hai* (glass in water is).

In an interrogative sentence the positions are as follows:

Where do you live?
āp kahān rahatē haiṅ?
you where live?

A simple question is often indicated by the tone and not by changing the placement of the verb as it is done in English. For example āpkā nām kyā hai? (What is your name?) is clear as an interrogation as indicated by kyā (What). But in a sentence such as āpkā nām Rām hai? (Is your name Ram?) the question is indicated only by the tone

Sometimes the meaning is changed if the syntax is changed. For example,

āp kyā khāengē? (What will you eat?)
kyā āp khāengē? (Will you eat?)

CHAPTER TWO

NOUNS संज्ञा *Sangyā*

Gender (लिंग *linga*)

There are only two genders in Hindi—masculine ((*puling* पुलिंग) and feminine (*strīling* स्त्रीलिंग). Gender is either based on sex (in the case of human beings and animals) or on usage. There are no hard and fast rules. According to the general rule, all words ending with the vowel ā are masculine and those ending with th vowel ī are feminine. Words ending in a consonant may be masculine or feminine. But there are many exceptions to the rule which you will learn as you go on. It may be pointed out here that the gender is the weakest point of Hindi grammar. This should not discourage learners as they should know at the very outset that if they take time in mastering the gender in Hindi, it is because of the arbitrary rules of the grammar which are established more or less by usage. Some examples of common masculine and feminine nouns are given here:

Masculine Nouns ending with the sound ā

रुपिया	*rupiyā*	rupee
केला	*kēlā*	banana
संतरा	*santarā*	orange
कमरा	*kamārā*	room
लड़का	*laṛkā*	boy
बेटा	*bēṭā*	son

Masculine Nouns ending with a consonant:

घर	*ghar*	home or house
मकान	*makān*	house
मंदिर	*mandir*	temple
चावल	*chāval*	rice
फल	*phal*	fruit
फूल	*phūl*	flower

Exceptional masculine nouns which end with the vowel sound ī

आदमी	*ādamī*	man

हाथी	*hāthī*	elephant
पानी	*pānī*	water
घी	*ghī*	clarified butter
पति	*pati*	husband

Feminine nouns ending with the vowel sound

लड़की	*laṛkī*	girl
बेटी	*bēṭī*	daughter
पत्नी	*patnī*	wife
चीनी	*chīnī*	sugar
साड़ी	*sāṛī*	saree

Feminine nouns ending with a consonant

औरत	*aurat*	woman
कलम	*kalam*	pen.
किताब	*kitāb*	book
मेज़	*mēz*	table

Feminine nouns ending with the vowel sound ā

हवा	*havā*	wind, air
दवा	*davā*	medicine

The absence of a neuter gender may cause some confusion in the mind of the learners, e.g., while *chāval* (rice) is masculine, *roṭī* (bread) is feminine, *kān* (ear) is masculine but *nāk* (nose) is feminine, *dānt*(teeth) is masculine but *jībh* (tongue) is feminine. Nouns belonging to the same subject or of the same group like the different parts of the body, or different fruits or vegetables have different genders. As pointed out earlier, this can be learnt only through regular and uninhibited practice in speaking and attentive hearing.

In most cases a masculine noun can be converted into a feminine noun by changing the ā into ī ending. Examples:

Masculine		Feminine	
लड़का	*laṛkā*	लड़की	*laṛkī*
बेटा	*bēṭā*	बेटी	*bēṭī*

Sometimes feminine gender is used to indicate the diminutive form of an object, e.g., थाल *thāl* (a big metal plate for eating) becomes थाली *thālī*; कटोरा *kaṭōrā* (a big bowl) becomes कटोरी *kaṭōrī* (a small bowl).

Number (वचन *vachan*)

In the case of common nouns, the plural form is formed by the following rules :

i) Masculine nouns ending with ā

Singular	Plural
(एकवचन *ekvachan*)	(बहुवचन *bahuvachan*)
लड़का *laṛkā* (boy)	लड़के *laṛkē* (boys)
बेटा *bēṭā* (son)	बेटे *bēṭē* (sons)

ii) Masculine nouns ending with a consonant or any other vowel except ā do not change in the plural form

आदमी	*ādamī*	man
चाकू	*chākū*	knife
सेब	*sēb*	apple
मकान	*makān*	house
फल	*phal*	fruit
फूल	*phūl*	flower

iii) Feminine nouns ending with ī change into the plural form by adding yañ in the end, e.g.

Singular	Plural
लड़की *laṛkī* (girl)	लड़कियां *laṛkiyāñ* (girls)
बेटी *bēṭī* (daughter)	बेटियां *bēṭiyañ* (daughters)

iv) Feminine nouns ending with a consonant change into the plural form by adding ēñ to the last consonant, e.g.

Singular	Plural
किताब *kitāb* (book)	किताबें *kitābeñ* (books)

औरत *aurat* (woman) औरतें *urateñ* (women)

The gender and the number of the subject govern the qualifying adjective and the verb. The adjective and the verb also decline accordingly (explained in detail in the chapters on adjectives and verbs). Let us make some simple sentences.

यह लड़का है	*yah laṛkā hai*	This is a boy.
यह लड़की है	*yah laṛkī hai*	This is a girl.
यह लड़का सुन्दर है	*yah laṛkā sundar hai*	This boy is handsome.
यह लड़की सुन्दर है	*yah laṛkī sundar hai*	This girl is pretty.
यह लड़का छोटा है	*yah laṛkā chhōtā hai*	This boy is small.
यह लड़की छोटी है	*yah laṛkī chhōṭī hai*	This girl is small.

Let us first get the construction of the sentence clear. *Yāh larka hai,* translated literally would mean *this boy is.* As explained in the beginning, the verb always comes at the end of a sentence

The adjective *sundar* did not change in the case of *larkī* as the word *sundar* ends with a consonant.

It does not decline with the number or gender. But the adjective *chhoṭā* became *chhōṭī* in the case of a girl because of the long *ā* ending. You will now understand how important the end sound is.

The auxiliary verbs *hai* (is) or *haiñ* (are) do not change with gender. Let us have some more sentences to make this point clear.

यह घर बड़ा है।	*yah ghar baṛā hai.*	This house is big.
ये घर बड़े हैं।	*yē ghar baṛē haiñ.*	These houses are big.
यह कमरा छोटा है।	*yah kamrā chhōṭā hai.*	This room is small.
ये कमरे छोटे हैं।	*yē kamrē chhōṭē haiñ.*	These rooms are small.
ये कमरे बड़े हैं।	*yē kamrē baṛē haiñ.*	These rooms are big.
यह रोटी है।	*yah rōṭī hai.*	This is a bread.
ये रोटियां हैं।	*yē rōṭiyañ haiñ.*	These are breads.
यह रोटी गरम है।	*yah rōṭī garam hai.*	This bread is hot.
ये रोटियां गरम हैं।	*yē rōṭiyāñ garam haiñ.*	These breads are hot.

यह रोटी गरम नहीं है।	*yah rōṭī garam nahin hai*	This bread is not hot.
ये रोटियां गरम नहीं हैं।	*yē rōṭiyāñ garam nahīñ haiñ.*	These breads are not hot.
पानी ठंडा है।	*pānī ṭhanḍā hai.*	The water is cold.
पानी ठंडा नहीं है।	*pānī ṭhanḍā nāhīñ hai.*	The water is not cold.
कमरा गरम है।	*kamarā garam hai.*	The room is hot.
कमरा गरम नहीं है।	*kamarā garam nahīñ hai*	The room is not hot.

Vocablary

गरम	*garam*	hot, warm				ठंडा	*ṭhanḍā*	cold
नहीं	*nahīñ*	not, no	है	*hai*	is	हैं	*haiñ*	are

Articles

Note that there are no definite or indefinite articles in Hindi. Also note the placing of *nahīñ* in the above sentences.

CHAPTER THREE

CASES AND CASE SIGNS

Declension

Masculine nouns ending in a consonant–singular

नौकर ने	*naukar nē*	servant (nominative)
नौकर को	*naukar kō*	to the servant
नौकर से	*naukar sē*	from the servant
नौकर के लिए	*naukar kē liyē*	for the servant
नौकर का	*naukar kā*	of the servant.

यह काम नौकर ने किया *yeh kām naukar nē kiyā*	The servant did this work.
नौकर को काम दीजिए *naukar kō kām dījiyē*	Give work to the servant.
नौकर से काम लीजिए *naukar sē kām lījiyē*	Take work from the servant.
नौकर के लिए बहुत काम है *naukar kē liyē bahut kām hai*	There is plenty of work for the servant.

यह नौकर का काम है *yah naukar kā kām hai*	This is the servant's job.

Plural

नौकरों ने	*naukarōñ nē*
नौकरों को	*naukarōñ kō*
नौकरों से	*naukarōñ sē*
नौकरों के लिए	*naukarōñ kē liyē*
नौकरों का	*naukarōñ kā*

नौकरों ने काम किया *naukarōñ nē kām kiyā*	Servants did the work.
नौकरों को काम दीजिए *naukarōñ kō kām dījiyē*	Give work to the servants.
नौकरों से काम लीजिए *naukarōñ sē kām lījiyē*	Take work from the servants.
नौकरों के लिए बहुत काम है *naukarōñ kē liyē bahut kām hai*	There is plenty of work for the servants.
यह नौकरों का काम है *yah naukarōñ kā kām hai*	This is servants' job.

Masculine nouns ending in ā—Singular

लड़के ने	*laṛkē nē*
लड़के को	*laṛkē kō*

लड़के से	*laṛkē sē*
लड़के के लिए	*laṛkē kē liyē*
लड़के का	*laṛkē kā*

लड़के ने काम किया *laṛkē nē kām kiya*	The boy did the work.
लड़के को काम दीजिए *laṛkē kō kām dījiyē*	Give work to the boy.
लड़के से काम लीजिए *laṛkē sē kām lījiyē*	Take work from the boy.
लड़के के लिए काम है *laṛkē kē liyē kām hai*	There is work for the boy.
यह लड़के का काम है *yah laṛkē kā kām hai*	This is the boy's work.

Plural

लड़कों ने काम किया *laṛkōñ nē kām kiyā*	The boys did the work.
लड़कों को काम दीजिए *laṛkōñ kō kām dījiyē*	Give work to the boys.
लड़कों से काम लीजिए *laṛkōñ sē kām lījiyē*	Take work from the boys.

लड़कों के लिए काम है *laṛkōn̄ kē liyē kām hai*	There is work for the boys.
यह काम लड़कों का है *yah kām laṛkōn̄ kā hai*	This is the boys' work.

Masculine nouns ending in ī—Singular

आदमी ने	*ādamī nē*
आदमी को	*ādamī kō*
आदमी से	*ādamī sē*
आदमी के लिए	*ādamī kē liyē*
आदमी का	*ādamī kā*

आदमी ने काम किया *ādamī nē kām kiya*	The man did the work.
आदमी को काम दीजिए *ādamī kō kām dījiye*	Give work to the man.
आदमी से काम लीजिए *ādamī sē kām lījiyē*	Take work from the man.
आदमी के लिए काम है *ādamī kē liyē kām hai*	There is work for the man.
यह आदमी का काम है *yah ādamī kā kām hai.*	This is the man's work.

Masculine nouns ending in u—Singular

गुरु ने	*guru nē*

गुरु को	*guru kō*
गुरु से	*guru sē*
गुरु के लिए	*guru kē liyē*
गुरु का	*guru kā*
गुरु ने किताब दी *guru nē kitāb dī*	The teacher gave the book.
गुरु को किताब दीजिए *guru kō kitāb dījiyē*	Give the book to the teacher.
गुरु से किताब लीजिए *guru sē kitab lījiyē*	Take the book from the *guru*.
किताब गुरु के लिए है *kitāb guru kē liyē hai*	The book is for the *guru*.
किताब गुरु की है *kitāb guru kī hai*	The book is *guru's*.

Plural

गुरुओं ने	*guruōñ nē*
गुरुओं को	*guruōñ kō*
गुरुओं से	*guruōñ sē*
गुरुओं के लिए	*guruōñ kē liyē*
गुरुओं का	*guruōñ kā*
गुरुओं ने किताबें दीं *guruōñ nē kitabēñ dī*	The teachers gave the books.
गुरुओं को किताबें दीजिए *guruōñ kō kitabēñ dijiyē*	Give the books to the teachers.

गुरुओं से किताबें लीजिए *guruōñ sē kitābēñ lījiyē*	Take the books from the teachers.
किताबें गुरुओं के लिए हैं *kitabēñ guruōñ kē liyē hai*	The books are for the teachers.

Feminine nouns ending in ī—Singular

लड़की ने	*laṛkī nē*
लड़की को	*laṛkī kō*
लड़की से	*laṛkī sē*
लड़की के लिए	*laṛkī kē liyē*
लड़की का	*laṛkī kā*

लड़की ने माला पहनी *laṛkī nē mālā pahanī*	The girl wore the garland.
लड़की को माला दीजिए *laṛkī kō mālā dījiyē*	Give the garland to the girl.
लड़की से माला लीजिए *laṛkī sē mālā lījiyē*	Take the garland from the girl.
माला लड़की के लिए है *mālā laṛki kē liyē hai*	The garland is for the girl.
माला लड़की की है *mālā laṛkī kī hai*	The garland is the girl's.

Plural

लड़कियों ने	*laṛkiyōñ nē*

लड़कियों को	*laṛkiyōñ kō*
लड़कियों से	*laṛkiyōñ sē*
लड़कियों के लिए	*laṛkiyōñ kē liyē*
लड़कियों का	*laṛkiyōñ kā*

लड़कियों ने मालाएं पहनीं *laṛkiyōñ nē mālāēñ pahanīñ*	The girls wore the garlands.
लड़कियों को मालाएँ दीजिए *larkiyōñ kō mālāēñ dījiyē*	Give the garlands to the girls.
लड़कियों से मालाएँ लीजिए *laṛkiyōñ sē mālāēñ lījiyē*	Take the garlands from the girls.
मालाएं लड़कियों के लिए हैं *mālāēñ larkiyōñ kē liyē haiñ*	The garlands are for the girls.
मालाएं लड़कियों की हैं *mālāēñ laṛkiyōñ kī haiñ*	The garlands are of the girls.

Feminine nouns ending in a consonant—Singular

औरत ने	*aurat nē*
औरत को	*aurat kō*
औरत से	*aurat sē*
औरत के लिए	*aurat kē liyē*
औरत का	*aurat kā*

औरत ने माला पहनी *aurat nē mālā pahanī*	The woman wore the garland.
औरत को माला दीजिए *aurat kō mālā dījiyē*	Give the garland to the woman.
औरत से माला लीजिए *aurat sē mālā lījiyē*	Take the garland from the woman.
माला औरत के लिए है *mālā aurat kē liyē hai*	The garland is for the woman.
माला औरत की है *mālā aurat kī hai*	The garland is the woman's.

Rules to remember

1. When there is a suffix to a noun which is the subject, the form of the verb changes not according to the subject, but according to the gender and number of the object.
2. When there is no suffix to the noun which is the subject, the form of the verb changes according to the subject.
3. If a masculine noun ends in *ā*, the ending changes into *ē* when there is a suffix.
4. If a masculine noun ends in ē in the plural form, the ending changes into *ōñ* when there is a suffix to it.

5. Feminine noun in the singular number does not change its form even when there is a suffix.
6. Feminine noun in the plural form having yāñ ending, changes into *yōñ* ending if there is a suffix.
7. Feminine nouns ending in a consonant or any other vowel in the plural, change into *ōñ* ending if there is a suffix.

CHAPTER FOUR

PRONOUN सर्वनाम *Sarvanam*

Personal Pronoun

First Person:	मैं	*māiñ*	I (M&F)
	हम	*hām*	we
	(pronounced as hum)		
	हम लोग	*ham lōg*	we people

(*lōg* is sometime added to clarify the plurality)

Second Person:	तुम	*tum*	you (M&F)
	तुम लोग	*tum lōg*	you people (M&F)
	आप	*āp*	you people (M&F)
	आप लोग	*āp lōg*	you people (M&F)
Third Person:	वह	*vah*	he, she, it, that

यह	*yah*	he, she, it, this
वे	*vē*	they
ये	*yē*	these

In nominative or objective case, personal pronouns, as seen above, change only with the person or number and not with the gender.

When the pronoun is the subject, the verb takes masculine or feminine, singular or plural form accordingly as it does in the case of a noun.

मैं जाता हूं	*māi jātā hūñ*	I go (M)
मैं जाती हूं	*māi jātī huñ*	I go (F)
हम जाते हैं	*ham jātē haīñ*	we go (M)
हम जाती हैं	*ham jātī haiñ*	we go (F)
तुम जाते हो	*tum jātē hō*	you go (M)
तुम जाती हो	*tum jātī hō*	you go (F)
तुम लोग जाते हो	*tum lōg jātē hō*	you people go
आप जाते हैं	*āp jātē haīñ*	you go (M)
आप जाती हैं	*āp jātī haīñ*	you go (F)
आप लोग जाते हैं	*āp lōg jātē haīñ*	you people go

वह जाता है	*vah jātā hai*	he goes
वह जाती है	*vah jāti hai*	she goes
वे जाते हैं	*vē jātē haiñ*	they go
वे जाती हैं	*vē jātī haiñ*	they go(F)

The verb *jātā* changes into *jāti*, according to the subject and is followed by the appropriate auxiliary verb.

Since the pronouns, *mai*, *tum*, *āp*, *vah* etc. are common for feminine and masculine it is indicated by the verb whether the subject is masculine or feminine.

There are two forms of personal pronoun in the second person—*tum* and *āp*. Usually *tum* is used for a person who is either very familiar or much younger in age. It is also often used for a person much below in social status. *āp* is the respectful form of address. It is also formal and used for people with whom one is not so familiar. Since one is likely to commit mistakes, which may sound impolite, it would be better always to use *āp*.

There is yet another form *tū*, (thou) which is either very familiar, and an expression of endearment or it is derrogatory, depending for whom it is used. God is sometimes addressed as *tū*. Itss *tū*. equivalent in English would be thou. It is better to avoid using *tū* to avoid using it in wrong places and for the wrong person!

Possessive Pronouns

Possessive pronouns differ with the first, second and third person. The decline according to the noun they qualify. For example, my brother would be *mērā bhāī* **and my sister would be** *mērī bahīn*, **Whether a man speaks or a woman. Similarly in the third person** *his dog* **or** *her dog* **would both be** *uskā kuttā* **since** *kuttā* **is masculine;** *his mother* **or** *her brother* **would both be** *usakī mā* **since** *mā* **is feminine. The first important step would be to learn the possessive pronouns by heart.**

मेरा, मेरी, मेरे	*mērā, mērī, mērē*	my, mine
हमारा, हमारी, हमारे	*hamārā, hamārī, hamārē*	our, ours
तुम्हारा, तुम्हारी, तुम्हारे	*tumhārā, tumhārī, tumhārē*	your, yours
आपका, आपकी, आपके	*āpkā, āpkī, āpkē*	your, yours
उसका, उसकी, उसके	*uskā, uskī, uskē*	his or her
उनका, उनकी, उनके	*unkā, unkī, unkē*	their, theirs

Case

Suffixes or *case-signs*

ने	*nē*	nominative case—in Present Perfect and Past Perfect
को	*kō*	to
से	*sē*	by you with from
के द्वारा	*kē dvārā*	by through you
के लिए	*kē liyē*	for
*का, की, के	*kā, kī, kē*	of
में	*me*	in, inside
पर	*par*	on, upon

When suffixed to personal pronouns:

First Person:

मैं	*mai̐*	I

मैंने	*mainē*	I (nominative case in present perfect and past perfect)
मेरा	*mērā*	my, mine
मुझको	*mujhkō*	to me
मुझसे	*mujhsē*	to me, from me also, with me
मुझसे मेरे द्वारा	*mujhsē* *mēṛē dvārā*	by me through me
मेरे लिए	*mērē līyē*	for me
मुझमें, मुझपर	*mujhmē,* *mujhpar*	in me, on me

Second Person:

तुम	*tum*	you
तुमने	*tumnē*	you (nominative)
तुम्हारा	*tumharā*	your, yours
तुमको	*tumkō*	to you
तुमसे	*tumsē*	from you

तुम्हारे द्वारा तुमसे	*tumharē dvārā* *tumsē*	by you through you
तुम्हारे लिए	*tumhārē liyē*	for you
तुममें, तुमपर	*tum mē̃, tum par*	in you, on you
आप	*āp*	you
आपने	*āpnē*	you (nominative)
आपका	*āpkā*	of , yours
आपको	*āpkō*	to you
आपसे	*āpsē*	from you
आप से, आपके द्वारा	*āpsē, āpkē dvārā*	by you, through you
आपके लिए	*āp kē liyē*	for you
आपमें, आप पर	*āp mēñ, āp par*	in you or you
वह	*vāh*	he, she, it, that
उसने	*usanē*	he, she (nominative)
उसका	*usakā*	his, hers, its
उसको	*usakō*	to him, to her, to it
उससे	*usasē*	from him, from her, from it

उससे	*usasē*	by him/her/it
उसके द्वारा	*usakē dvārā*	through him her/it
उसके लिए	*usakē liyē*	for him/her/it
उसमें, उसपर	*usamē, usapar*	in him, on him/her/it
वे	*vē*	they
उन्होंने	*unhōññē*	they (nominative)
उनका	*unakā*	their, theirs
उनको	*unakō*	to them
उनसे	*unasē*	from them
उनसे उनके द्वारा	*unasē* *unakē dvārā*	by them, through them
उनके लिए	*unakē liyē*	for them
उनमें, उन पर	*unamēñ, unpar*	in them, on them

Examples :

मैंने रोटी खाई	*mainē rōṭi khāyī*	I ate bread.
यह मेरा घर है	*yeh mērā ghar hai*	This is my house.
किताब मुझको दीजिए	*kitāb mujhkō dījiyē*	Give the book to me.

मुझसे यह काम नहीं होगा	*mujhasē yah kām nahī hōgā*	This work cannot be done by me.
आप मेरे लिए क्या लाए हैं?	*āp mērē liyē kyā lāyē haīñ*	What have you brought for me?
मुझसे आपको क्या चाहिए?	*mujhasē āpkō kyā chāhīyē*	What do you want from me?
मेरी बेटी घर में है	*mērī bētī ghar mēñ hai*	My daughter is in the house.
मुझमें ताकत नहीं है	*mujhamē ta-kat nahī hai*	There is no strength in me.
मुझ पर दया कीजिए	*mujh par dayā kījiyē*	Have pity on me.

Second Person :

*तुमने रोटी खाई?	*tumnē rōtī khāyī?*	Have you eaten bread? (meal)
तुम्हारा घर कहां है?	*tumhārā ghar kahāñ haī?*	Where is your house?
तुमको पत्र किसने दिया?	*tūmkō patra kisnē diyā?*	Who gave you the letter?

---

*In the north India when a person speaks of eating *roti* he often means eating a meal.

वह तुमसे कितने रुपए मांगता है?	*Vah tumsē kitanē rupayē māngtā hai?*	How many rupees is he asking from you?
तुमसे उसका काम हो सकेगा?	*tumsē usakā kām hō sakēgā?*	Can his work be done by you?
वह तुम्हारे लिए क्या लाया है?	*vah tūmharē liyē kyā lāyā hai?*	What has he brought for you?
उसको तुम पर भरोसा है?	*uskō tum par bharōsā hai.*	He has trust on you.

(In Hindi it is not trust *in* someone, but *on* someone.)

आपने क्या कहा?	*āpnē kyā kahā?*	What did you say?
आपका शुभ नाम क्या है ?	*āpkā shubh nām kyā hai?*	What is your auspicious name?

(It is not very polite to ask *āpkā nām kyā hai*? Many Indians wrongly translate this literally into English as : What is your good name?)

आपको क्या चाहिए?	*āpkō kyā chāhiyē?*	What do you want?

मुझको आपसे एक किताब चाहिए	*mujhkō āpsē ēk kitāb chāhiyē*	I want a book from you.
आपसे यह काम होगा?	*āpsē yah kām hōga?*	Can this work be done by you?
मैं आपके लिए फूल लायी हूं	*maiñ āpkē liyē phūl lāyī hūñ*	I have brought flowers for you.
आपमें बहुत गुण हैं	*āpmēñ bahut guṇ haiñ*	You have many good qualities.
मुझको आप पर भरोसा है	*mujhkō āp par bharōsā hai*	I have trust in you.

Third Person:

उसने क्या कहा था?	*usanē kyā kahā thā?*	What did he say?
उसका घर कहां है?	*usakā ghar kahāñ hai?*	Where is his house?
उसको क्या चाहिए?	*usako kyā chāhiyē?*	What does he want?
उससे रुपये मांगो	*usasē rūpayē māngō*	Ask money from him.

उससे यह काम नहीं हो सकता	*usasē yah kām nāhīñ hō sakatā*	This work cannot be done by him.
मैं उसके लिए खाना लाता हूं	*maīñ usakē liyē khānā lata hūñ*	I bring food for him.
मेरे कपड़े उसमें नहीं हैं	*mērē kapṛē usmēñ nahīñ haīñ*	My clothes are not in that.
इस पर किताबें मत रखो	*is per kitābēñ mat rakhō*	Don't keep the books on this.

In the case of the third person the pronouns *us* or *un* may be used to qualify a noun, e.g., *on that table—us mez par*; in this cupboard—*is almārī meñ*. As prepositions are actually postpositions in Hindi, they are placed *after* and *not before*—a noun or pronoun.

More Examples:

मेरी किताबें उस अलमारी में हैं	*mērī kitābēñ us almārī mēñ haīñ*	My books are in that cupboard.

राम इस घर में रहता है	*Ram is ghar mēñ rahtā hai*	Ram lives in this house.
सीता उस स्कूल में पढ़ाती है	*Sita us skūl mēñ parhātı hai*	Sita teaches in that school.
प्याले उस मेज़ पर रखो	*pyālē us mēz par rākhō*	Put the cups on that table.
उस कमरे को साफ़ करो	*us kamarē kō sāf karō*	Clean that room.
रुपए उस जेब में है	*rupaẏē us jēb mēñ hai*	Money is in that pocket.

New Words :

tākat	strength	*dayā*	pity
kıjiyē	please do	*patra*	letter
māngtā	asks for	*lāyā*	has brought
bharōsā	trust	*shubh*	auspicious, good
guṇ	virtues	*almārı*	cupboard
paṛhātı hāi	teaches	*jēb*	pocket

CHAPTER FIVE

PREPOSITIONS

A preposition, as already explained, is actually a postposition in Hindi as it occurs not before but *after* a noun or pronoun. For example, *on the table* would be *table on* and *in the room* would be *room in*. *The book is on the table* would be *the book table on is (Kitab mēz par hai)*.

Post-positions or case-signs

ने	*ne*	(nominative case—present perfect and past perfect)
का, की, के	*kā, kī, kē*	of
को	*kō*	to
से	*sē*	from, with and by
पर	*par*	on, above
में	*mēñ*	in

Prepositions in Hindi are suffixes to pronouns, but they are written as a separate word with nouns. Example :

Ram ko but *mujhkō* (to me)

mēz par	but	*uspār*	(on that)
kamarē mēñ	but	*usmēñ*	(in that)
Ram nē	but	*māñinē*	(I)

Ke sāth is also used when the meaning is together with or in the company of.

For example—*I shall go with you* would be *maīñ āpkē sāth jāungā.* But *I write with a pen* would be *maiñ kalam sē likhatā hūñ. I wash clothes with soap* would be *maiñ sābun sē kapṛē dhōtā hūñ.*

Further Examples,:

He eats with a spoon—*Vah chammach sē khātā hai.*

He cuts the mango with the knife—*Vah chhurī sē ām kāṭatā hai.*

When a noun is not followed by a post-position or a case-sign, it changes from singular to plural as already explained in detail in the Chapter on nouns. But if it is followed by a post-position, it changes by adding *ē* to the masculine singular, and *ōñ* to masculine plural. In the case of feminine nouns, there is no change in the case of singular but *ōñ* is added in the end for plural. Examples :

Without post-position :

Singular		Plural	
कमरा	*kamarā* (M)	कमरे	*kamarē*
कुरसी	*kursī* (F)	कुरसियाँ	*kursiyāñ*

With post-position :

Singular		Plural	
कमरे में	*kamarē mē*	कमरों में	*kamarōñ mēñ*
कुरसी पर	*kursī par*	कुरसियों पर	*kursiōñ par*

कमरा साफ़ है	*kamarā sāf hāi*	The room is clean.
कमरे साफ़ हैं	*kamarē sāf hāiñ*	The rooms are clean.

With post-position :

कमरे में गरमी है	*kamarē mēñ garamī hai*	It is hot in the room.
कमरों में गरमी है	*kamarōñ mēñ garamī hai*	It is hot in the rooms.

घर में जाले हैं	*ghar mēñ jālē hāiñ*	There are cobwebs in the house.
घरों में जाले हैं	*ghrōñ mēñ jālē hāiñ*	There are cobwebs in the houses.

Another example (feminine noun) :

मेज़ पर किताब है	*mēz par kitāb hai*	The book is on the a table.
मेज़ों पर किताबें हैं	*mēzōñ par kitābēñ hāiñ*	Books are on the tables.
कुरसी पर धूल है	*kursī par dhūl hai*	There is dust on the chair.
कुरसियों पर धूल है	*kursiyōñ par dhūl hai*	There is dust on the chairs.

Reading Exercise :

छोटा चम्मच प्याले में है	*choṭā chammach pyālē mēñ hai.*	The small spoon is in the cup.
प्यालों में चम्मच नहीं हैं	*pyaloñ mēñ chammach nahīñ hāiñ*	There are no spoons in the cups.

मेरा कुत्ता बीमार है	*mērā Kuttā bimār hai*	My dog is sick.
कुत्ते को डाक्टर के पास ले जाइए	*kuttē kō doctor kē pās lē jāiyē.*	Please take the dog to the doctor.
कुत्ते के लिए दवा लाइए	*kuttē kē liyē davā lāiyē*	Please bring medicine for the dog.
अपने कुत्तों को यहां मत लाइए।	*apanē kuttoñ kō yahāñ mat lāiyē*	Please don't bring your dogs here.
सड़क पर बहुत पानी है	*saṛak par bahut pānī hai*	There is a lot of water on the road.
सड़कों पर बहुत पानी है	*saṛkōñ par bahut pānī hai*	There is a lot of water on the roads.
इस शीशे को साफ़ करो	*is shīshē kō sāf karō*	Clean this mirror.
*इन शीशों को साफ करो	*in shīshōñ kō sāf karō*	Clean these mirrors.

*** This can be said without the post-position—*vah shīshā sāf karō* But when the post-position *kō* is used *shīshā* becomes *shīshē*.**

CHAPTER SIX

ADJECTIVE विशेषण *Visheshaṇ*

यह गोरा लड़का है	*yah gōrā laṛkā hai*	This boy is fair.
ये गोरे लड़के हैं	*yē gōrē laṛkē haiñ*	These boys are fair.
यह गोरी लड़की है	*yah gōrī laṛkī hai*	This girl is fair.
ये गोरी लड़कियाँ हैं	*ye gōrī laṛkiyāñ haiñ*	These girls are fair.
यह बड़ा घर है	*yah baṛā ghar hai*	This is a big house.
ये बड़े घर हैं	*yē baṛē ghar haiñ*	These are big houses.
यह बड़ी मेज़ है	*yah baṛī mēz hai*	This is a big table.
ये बड़ी मेज़ें हैं	*ye baṛī mēzēñ haiñ*	These are big tables.

1. If an adjective ends with *ā* sound, it declines according to the number and gender of the noun it qualifies. In the first set of sentences above, the noun *laṛkā* and the qualifying adjective

gōrā both have *ā* ending and decline But it would also be noticed that in the case of feminine plural, the adjective does not change its form, e.g. *laṛkiyāñ gōrī hāiñ*.

2. In the second set of sentences, while the adjective *baṛā* ends in *ā*, the nouns *ghar* and *mēz* end in a consonant. But the adjective declines as it does in the first set of sentences. The second rule to remember, therefore, is : *an adjective ending in ā sound will change its ending according to the number and gender of the noun it qualifies even if the noun does not end in ā sound.* Some more examples would clarify the point further.

मीठा केला	*mīṭhā kēlā*	sweet banana
मीठे केले	*mīṭhē kēlē*	sweet bananas
मीठी नारंगी	*mīṭhī nārangī*	sweet tangarine
मीठी नारंगियां	*mīṭhī nārangiyāñ*	sweet tangarines

Here the masculine as well as the feminine nouns rhyme with the adjective.

मोटा आदमी	*mōṭā adamī*	fat man
मोटे आदमी	*moṭē ādamī*	fat men
मोटी औरत	*moṭī aurat*	fat woman
मोटी औरतें	*mōṭi auratēñ*	fat women
अच्छा शहर	*achchhā shahar*	good city
अच्छे शहर	*achchhē shahar*	good cities
अच्छी जगह	*achchhī jagah*	good place
अच्छी जगहें	*achchhi jaghēñ*	good places

In the examples given above the nouns *shahar* and *jagah* have consonant ending, but the adjective decline all the same since they have ā ending.

3. If the adjective does not have ā ending, it *never* changes its form. Example:

वीर लड़का	*vīr laṛkā*	brave boy
वीर लड़के	*vīr laṛkē*	brave boys
वीर लड़की	*vīr laṛkī*	brave girl
वीर लड़कियां	*vīr laṛkiyāñ*	brave girls
गरम पकौड़ा	*garam pakōṛā*	hot pakora
गरम पकौड़े	*garam pakōṛē*	hot pakoras
गरम रोटी	*garam rōṭī*	hot roti
गरम रोटियां	*garam rōṭiyāñ*	hot rotis

4. There are some other rules of usage which should be remembered.

(1) **Words indicating the proression of a person have a masculine gender even if the last syllable of the word is ī, e. g., *mālī* (gardener); *nā-ī* (barber); *kasā-ī* (butcher); *dhobī* (washerman).**

(2) Names of rivers are always of the feminine gender.

(3) Names of the days of the week are of masculine gender.

(4) Certain birds and animals such as *kōyal* (cuckoo), *battakh* (duck), *gilahrī* (squirrel), *lomṛī* (fox) are always used in the feminine gender.

Certain other animals such as *bhēṛiyā* (wolf), *chītā* (cheetah), *tēnduā* (leopard) are always treated as masculine gender.

Sometimes when the subject is in plural the adjective is repeated for emphasis and good expression, e.g.,

सुन्दर सुन्दर फूल	*sundar-sundar phul*	beautiful flowers
बड़े-बड़े मकान	*baṛē-baṛē makān*	big houses
गरम गरम रोटियाँ	*garam-garam rōṭiyāñ*	hot bread
मीठे मीठे फल	*miṭhē-miṭhē phal*	sweet fruits

There are some adjectives which do not change form with change in number or gender. For Example :

अमीर	*amīr*	rich
गरीब	*garīb*	poor
जवान	*jawān*	young

खराब	*kharāb*	bad, poor in quality
खूबसूरत	*khūbsūrat*	beautiful
बढ़िया	*baṛhiyā*	excellent, of high quality
ईमानदार	*īmandār*	honest
बेईमान	*bēimān*	dishonest
सुस्त	*sust*	dull
तेज़	*tēz*	sharp
चालाक	*chālāk*	cunning

These adjectives are originally derived from Urdu but now adopted in Hindi like hundreds of other Urdu words and are a part of the spoken Hindi now.

Let us use them into sentences.

यह आदमी अमीर है	*yah ādamī amīr hai*	This man is rich.
यह औरत अमीर है	*yah aurat amīr hai*	This woman is rich.
ये लोग गरीब हैं	*yē lōg garīb haiñ*	These people are poor.
मैं गरीब हूँ	*maiñ garīb hūñ*	I am poor.
यह लड़का जवान है	*yah laṛkā jawān hai*	This boy is young.
ये लड़कियां जवान है	*yē laṛkiyāñ jawān haiñ*	These girls are young.
यह शहर खूबसूरत है	*yah shahar khūbsūrat hai*	This city is beautiful.
ये फूल खूबसूरत हैं	*yē phūl khūbsūrat haiñ*	These flowers are beautiful.
मेरा माली ईमानदार है	*mērā māli imāndār hai*	My gardener is honest.
मेरा दूधवाला बेईमान है	*mērā dūdhwālā beimān hai*	My milkman is dishonest.

यह छुरी तेज है	*yah chhurī tēz hai*	This knife is sharp.
ये छुरियां तेज हैं	*yē chhuriāñ tēz haīñ*	These knives are sharp.

The three degrees of an adjective are denoted by adding words to the basic words, e.g.,

Positive	**Comparative**	**Superlative**
achchhā (good)	*usasē achchhā* (better)	*sabsē achchhā* (best)
kharāb (bad)	*usa sē kharāb* (worse)	*sabsē kharāb* (worst)
sundar (pretty)	*usasē sunder* (prettier)	*sabsē sundar* (prettiest)

The examples given for comparative degree, mean better than that, worse than that, or prettier than that. A more concrete comparison would be :

राम अच्छा लड़का है।	*Ram achchhā laṛkā hai*	Ram is a good boy.
श्याम राम से अच्छा है।	*Shyam Ram sē achchhā hai*	Shyam is better than Ram.
हरी सबसे अच्छा लड़का है।	*Harī sabsē achchhā laṛkā hai*	Hari is the best boy.

Some more examples :

कलकत्ता भारत का सबसे बड़ा शहर है।	*Kalkattā Bharat kā sabsē baṛā shahār haī*	Calcutta is the biggest city of India.

(Literally *sabse barā* means, bigger than all.)

गुलाब सबसे सुन्दर फूल है	*Gulāb sabsē sundar phūl hai*	Rose is the prettiest flower.
राम श्याम से ज्यादा होशियार है।	*Ram Shyam sē zyādā hōshiyār hai*	Ram is more intelligent than Shyam.
कक्षा में राम सबसे ज्यादा होशियार है।	*Kakshā mēñ Ram sabsē zyādā hōshiyār hai*	Ram is most intelligent in the class.

Sometimes superlatives are also expressed in the following manner :

अच्छे से अच्छा	*achchhē sē achchhā*	best
खराब से खराब	*kharāb sē kharāb*	worst
मज़बूत से मज़बूत	*mazbūt sē mazbūt*	strongest
कमजोर से कमज़ोर	*kamzōr sē kamzōr*	weakest

Adjectives in pairs :

Two adjectives having similarity in meaning are used as one phrase for emphasis. For example :

साफ-सुथरा	*sāf-sutharā*	neat and clean
मैला-कुचैला	*mailā-kuchailā*	very filthy

(The word *kuchailā* is never used by itself.)

सड़ा-गला	*saṛā-galā*	very rotten
आपका घर कितना साफ़-सुथरा है	*āpkā ghar kitnā sāf-suthara hāi*	How clean is your house !

Some more examples :

मेरा काला कोट कहां है ?	*mērā kālā kōṭ kahāñ hai?*	Where is my black coat?
यह कोट तो मैला है	*yah kōt tō mailā hai*	This coat is dirty.
यह धोबी अच्छा नहीं है	*yah dhōbī achchhā nahīñ hai*	This washerman is not good.
यह रोटी बिल्कुल ठंडी है	*yah rōṭī bilkul ṭhanḍī hai*	This roti is absolutely cold.
गरम रोटी लाइए	*garam rōṭī lāiyē*	Please bring hot bread.
ये आम बिल्कुल खट्टे हैं	*yē ām bilkul khaṭṭē haiñ*	These mangoes are absolutely sour.
मीठे-मीठे आम लाइए	*mīṭhē-mīṭhē ām lāiyē*	Please bring sweet mangoes.
आपकी यह आदत बहुत बुरी है	*āpkī yah ādat bahut burī hai*	This habit of yours is very bad.

बच्चों की आदतें अच्छी नहीं हैं	*bachchōñ kī adatēñ achchhī nahīñ hāiñ*	Children's habits are not good.
आपकी हरी साड़ी सुन्दर है	*apkī harī saṛī sundar hai*	Your green sari is pretty.
क्या बहुत महंगी है ?	*kyā bahut mahangī hai?*	Is it very expensive?
जी नहीं, बहुत महंगी नहीं है	*ji nahīñ, bahut mahangī nahiñ hai*	No, it is not very expensive.
आज कमरा साफ़ नहीं है	*āj kamarā sāf nahīñ hai*	Today the room is not clean.
जमादार बहुत सुस्त है	*jamādār bahut sust hai*	Jamadar (sweeper) is very lazy
वह बेचारा बीमार है	*vah bēchārā bīmār hai*	The poor fellow is sick.
वह बहुत लापरवाह है	*vah bahut lāparvāh hai*	He is very careless.
उसके बच्चे बहुत दुबले-पतले हैं	*usakē bachchē bahut dubalē-patlē haīñ*	His children are very lean and thin.

वे कमज़ोर हैं क्योंकि काफ़ी दूध नहीं पीते।	*vē kamzōr haiñ kyōnki kafī dūdh nahīñ pītē*	They are weak because they don't drink enough milk.
यह दुकान बहुत महंगी है	*vah dukān bahut mahangī hai*	This shop is very expensive.
दूसरी दुकान कम महंगी है	*dūsarī dūkān kam mahangī hai*	The other shop is less expensive.
वह दुकानदार ईमानदार है	*vah dukāndār īmāndār hai*	That shopkeeper is honest.

New words in this chapter

मैला	*mailā*	dirty
धोबी	*dhōbī*	washerman
बिल्कुल	*bilkul*	absolutely
ठंडी	*ṭhanḍī*	cold
लाइए	*la-iyē*	please bring

khaṭṭā	sour	*miṭhē-miṭhē*	sweet (note the repetition of the word for emphasis, also denoting selectivity)
ādat (F)	habit		
harī	green		
mahangī	expensive		
sāf	clean		
sust	lazy, inactive, slow	*lāparvāh*	careless
		dubalē-patalē	lean and thin (double adjective for emphasis and expression)
kāfī	enough		
pītē	drink		
dūkān	shop		
**kam*	less	*dūkāndar*	shopkeeper

*कम ***kam*** should not be confused with काम ***kām***. The former *means* less and the latter means work. So *kam kām* would mean less work.

CHAPTER SEVEN

VERB क्रिया *Kriyā*

The verb is the most important part of a sentence. Grammatically speaking If you have mastered the verb, you have mastered the language. Here we shall explain the basic forms of the verb without giving the tongue-twisting names of its various forms.

As in English, there are three tenses (*kāl*) in Hindi too—Present, Future and Past— *vartamān bhavishya and bhūt*

The auxiliary verbs, which have already been introduced in the chapter on pronouns, are given here again for not only refreshing your memory but for memorising them.

They are extremely important.

हूं	*hūṅ*	am
है	*hai*	is
हैं	*haiṅ*	are
था, थी	*thā, thī*	was
थे, थीं	*thē, thīṅ*	were
गा, गी, गे	*gā, gī, gē*	will, shall

As already explained earlier, the *verb always comes last in a sentence and the auxiliary verb comes at the very end. In an interrogative* sentence *the verb does not change its place.* The interrogation is indicated by the tone of the speech. For example:

आपका नाम राम है।	Your name is Ram.
āpkā nām Ram hai.	
आपका नाम राम है?	Your name is Ram?
āpkā nām Ram hai?	

Sometimes a question may be emphasised by adding *kya* (what) at the beginning.

क्या आपका नाम राम है ?	Is your name Ram?
Kyā āpkā nām Ram hai ?	

Tenses : Present Indefinite

मैं जाता हूं	*maīñ jatā hūñ*	I go (M)
मैं जाती हूं	*maīñ jāti hūñ*	I go (F)
हम जाते हैं	*ham jātē hāiñ*	We go
तुम जाते हो	*tum jātē hō*	You go
तुम जाती हो	*tum jātī hō*	You go (F)
आप जाते हैं	*āp jātē hāīñ*	You go
आप जाती हैं	*āp jātī hāīñ*	You go (F)
वह जाता है	*vah jātā hai*	He goes.

वह जाती है	*vah jātī hai*	She goes
वे जाते हैं	*vē jātē hāīñ*	They go
वे जातीं हैं	*vē jātī hāīñ*	They go (F)

The sentences given above are in the Present Indefinite tense. It is formed by adding *tā, tī* or *tē* to the root of the verb, depending on the gender and the number of the subject, and adding the proper auxilliary verb in the end. For example, take the first sentence. The root of the verb *jātā* is *jā*. If the subject is masculine singular, *tā* is added to the root making it *jātā*. Similarly in the second sentence *tī* has been added to *ā* making it *ātī* as the subject is feminine. The form of the verb, therefore, depends not only on the tense and mood but also on the subject.

Let us take another verb, *pīnā* (to drink). We shall first take nouns as subjects and then pronouns.

Ram kyā pītā hai?	What does Ram drink?
Ram dūdh pītā hai	Ram drinks milk.
Sita kyā pītī hai?	What does Sita drink?
Sita pānī pītī hai	Sita drinks water.
Ram aur Sita chāe pītē hāīñ?	Ram and Sita drink tea?

Jī hāñ, Ram aur Sita chāe pitē hāīñ	Yes, Ram and Sita drink tea.
Ram aur Sita chāe nahīñ pītē, dūdh pītē hāīñ	Ram and Sita do not drink tea, they drink milk.

Several points can be noticed in the sentences given above.

1. *Since the verb* pīnā *is transitive, there is an object in every sentence* which does not affect the verb.
2. *The verb is still governed by the subject, whether noun or pronoun.*
3. *The sentence* jī hāñ Ram aur Sita chāe pītē haiñ *has two subjects, one masculine, the other feminine. In such cases, the verb will be* masculine plural.
4. *The last sentence is a compound sentence.*

The first sentence is negative, *Ram aur Sitā chāe nahī pītē haīñ,Jīhāñ*(Yes) is added for emphasis and clarity. *Jī* is added for politeness like saying 'Yes, please.'

Now, if the subject is a pronoun :

māī khātā hūñ	I eat.
māī khātī hūñ	I eat. (F)
ham khātē hāīñ	We eat.

Tum khātē hō	You eat.
Tum khātī hō	You eat. (F)
Tum lōg khātē hō	You (people) eat.
āp khātē haīñ	You eat.
āp khātī haīñ	You eat. (F)
āp lōg khātē haīñ	You (people) eat.
vah khātē haīñ	He eats.
vah khātī hāī	She eats.
vē khātē haīñ	They eat.
vē khātī haīñ	They eat. (F)

It is advisable to read aloud this table to understand clearly and to memorize the rules by which the form of a verb is changed. A list of verbs of common usage is given at the end of the book. The reader is advised to take a few words and form sentences based on the examples given here. But the most important thing is to use what you learn. If you commit mistakes, which you will in the early stages, they will get corrected in the process and you will be able to express yourself clearly and confidently. *The first thing one must give up while learning a language is inhibition.*

Present Continuous

मैं जा रहा हूं	*maiñ jā rahā hūñ*	I am going. (M)
मैं जा रही हूं	*maiñ jā rahī hūñ*	I am going. (F)
हम जा रहे हैं	*ham jā rahē haiñ*	We are going.
तुम जा रहे हो	*tum jā rahē hō*	You are going. (M)
तुम जा रही हो	*tum jā rāhī hō*	You are going. (F)
श्राप जा रहे हैं	*āp jā rahē haiñ*	You are going. (M)
श्राप जा रही हैं	*āp jā rahi haiñ*	You are going. (F)
श्राप लोग जा रहे हैं	*āp lōg jā rahē haiñ*	You (people) are going.
वह जा रहा है	*vah jā rahā hai*	He is going.
वे जा रहे हैं	*vē jā rahē haiñ*	They are going. (M)
वे जा रही हैं	*vē jā rahī haiñ*	They are going. (F)

Although the familiar and informal form of address, *tum* has been given throughout this book, readers are advised to use only *āp* as far as possible, not only to make learning simpler and easier, but also to avoid any possible embarrassment, for unless you are very familiar with the person, or he or she is much younger to you, *tum* may sound impolite and may mean disrespect.

Even when referring to a third person who is not present, it would be advisable to use the verb in the third person plural to show respect. For instance, if you are referring to the President of India (*Rashtrapati*), it would be very impolite and discourteous to say *Rashtrapati ā rahā hai.* The proper form would be *Rashtrapati ā rahē haiñ.*

The point to remember is that the plural form of a verb, when the subject is second or third person, is the polite form and, therefore, safer to use.

Similarly, if you are referring to someone's parents, husband or wife, courtesy demands to use the plural form of the verb. For Example:

āpkē pati kaisē haiñ? How is your husband?
āpkī patnī kaisī haiñ? How is your wife?

and not *āpkā pati kaisā hai* or *āpkī patnī kaisī hai.*

Please also note that the possessive pronoun *āpkā* also takes the plural form *āpkē* to coincide with the plural form of the verb.

Present Perfect

When a job has been completed now or in the very near past, the verb is in the present perfect. But in this form there is a variation in the rules regarding Transitive verbs and intransitive verbs. We shall first take an example of an intransitive verb—ānā (to come).

To get the Present Perfect form ā, ā-ī, ā-ē, is added to the root of the principal verb which is followed by the auxiliary verb.

मैं आया हूं	*maiñ āyā hūñ*	I have come.
मैं आई हूं	*maiñ āyī hūñ*	I have come. (F)
हम आए हैं	*ham āyē haiñ*	We have come. (F & M)
तुम आए हो	*tum āyē hō*	You have come.
तुम आई हो	*tum āyī hō*	You have come. (F)
आप आए हैं	*āp āyē haiñ*	You have come.
आप आई हैं	*āp āyī haiñ*	You have come. (F)
आप लोग आए हैं	*āp lōg āyē haiñ*	You (people) have come.

वह आया है	*vah āyā hai*	He has come.
वह आई है	*vah āyī hai*	She has come.
वे आए हैं	*vē āyē haiñ*	They have come
वे आई हैं	*vē āyī haiñ*	They have come. (F)

When the verb is transitive, *nē* is added as a suffix to the subject—noun or pronoun. Study the sentences given below as examples and read them aloud several times.

मैंने खाया है	*mainē khāyā hai*	I have eaten.
हमने खाया है	*hamnē khāyā hai*	We have eaten.
तुमने खाया है	*tumnē khāyā hai*	You have eaten.
आपने खाया है	*āpnē khāyā hai*	You have eaten.
उसने खाया है	*usnē khāyā hai*	He/She has eaten.
उन्होंने खाया है	*unhōnē khāyā hai*	They have eaten.

The verbs, both the principal and the auxiliary have not changed with the person, number or gender even though the object has not been mentioned.

When the object is not mentioned, the transitive verb is always in the masculine singular form.

More examples :

मैंने पिया है	*mainē piyā hai*	I have drunk.
हमने पिया है	*hamnē piyā hai*	We have drunk.
तुमने पिया है	*tumnē piyā hai*	You have drunk.
उसने पिया है	*usnē piyā hai*	He/She has drunk.
उन्होने पिया है	*unhōnē piyā hai*	They have drunk.

The important points to remember in the case of he present perfect are:

(i) **ने *nē* is added as a suffix to the subject--noun or pronoun.**

(ii) **the verb does not change with the subject.**

(iii) **the verb changes with the object.**

मैंने रोटी खाई	*mainē rōṭī khāyī*	I ate bread.
आपने रोटियां खाईं	*āpnē rōṭiyāñ khāyī*	You ate breads.
मैंने केला खाया	*mainē kēlā khāyā*	I ate banana.
तुमने आम खाए	*tumnē ām khāyē*	You ate mangoes

उसने संतरे खाए	*usane santarē khāyē*	He ate oranges.
उसने मछली खाई	*usanē machhli khāyī*	He ate fish

In the sentences given above the verb *khāyā* has changed throughout according to the number and gender of the objects—roṭī, roṭiyāñ, kēlā, ām, santarē, machhli, etc.

There are some irregular verbs which change differently for present perfect. They are jānā (to go), dēnā (to give) and karnā (to do).

jānā becomes *gayā* instead of jaya.
maiñ gayā, ap gayē, vah gayā and so on.
Dēnā becomes *diyā* instead of *deya.*
Karnā becomes *kiyā* and not *karya.*

The last two are transitive verbs.

Note: खाई has been spelt here in Roman script as *khayī* and not *khāī*, although phonetically the latter spelling would be correct. This has been done to avoid confusion regarding pronunciation. *ā* and *ī* here are two syllables, but are likely to be read as the vowel *ai*, unless the two vowels are separated by a hyphen. This spelling in the Roman script appears more logical and easier to remember and to pronounce. In Hindi some people write it as आयी or आये which also is correct.

Present Perfect Continuous

मैं जाता रहा हूं	*maiñ jātā rahā hūñ*	I have been going.
मैं आप से कहता रहा हूं	*maiñ āpsē kahtā rahā hūñ*	I have been telling you.
वह आता रहा है	*vah ātā rahā hai*	He has been coming.

Past Tense

Past Indefinite

मैं जाता था	*maiñ jātā thā*	I went.
मैं जाती थी	*maiñ jātī thī*	I went.
हम जाते थे	*ham jātē thē*	We went.
तुम जाते थे	*tum jātē thē*	You went.
आप जाते थे	*āp jātē thē*	You went.
वह जाता था	*vah jātā thā*	He went.
वह जाती थी	*vah jātī thī*	She went.
वे जाते थे	*vē jātē thē*	They went.

In the case of past indefinite, it is easier to remember the last auxiliary verbs as they follow a simpler pattern:

masculine singular	—	thā	(was)
masculine plural	—	thē	(were)
feminine singular	—	thī	(was)
feminine plural	—	thīn	(were)

Second person, of course, is always in plural.

Let us have more complete sentences:

दिल्ली में मैं स्कूल जाता था *Dillī mē maiñ skūl jātā thā*	I went to school in Delhi.
गरमी में हम सैर करते थे। *garmī mē ham sair kartē thē*	We went for walks in summer.
वह सिर्फ इतवार को आती थी। *vah sirf itvār kō ātī thī*	She came only on Sundays.
आप दिल्ली में क्या करते थे ? *āp Dillī mē kyā kartē thē?*	What did you do in Delhi?
मैं दिल्ली में पढ़ता था। *maiñ Dillī mē paṛhtā thā*	I studied in Delhi.
आप क्या पढ़ते थे ? *āp kyā paṛhtē thē?*	What did you study?
मैं हिन्दी पढ़ता था। *maiñ Hindī paṛhtā thā*	I studied Hindi.
आप हिन्दी कहाँ पढ़ते थे? *āp Hindī kahāñ paṛhtē thē?*	Where did yo study Hindi?

मैं विश्वविद्यालय में पढ़ता था। *maiñ vishva vidyālaya mē paṛhtā thā*	I studied in the University.
पिछले साल मैं भी दिल्ली में था। *pichhalē sāl maiñ bhī Dillī mē thā*	Last year I was also in Delhi.
क्या आप भी पढ़ते थे ? *kyā āp bhī paṛhtē thē?*	Did you study too?
जी नहीं, मैं नौकरी करता था। *jī nahī, maiñ naukarī kartā thā*	No, I was doing service.
आप कहाँ नौकरी करते थे ? *āp kahāñ naukarī kartē thē?*	Where did you serve? Where did you work?
मैं सरकारी अफसर था। *maiñ sarkārī afsar thā*	I was a government officer.

New words appearing in this lesson:

kyā	what
paṛhnā	to study, to read
kahāñ	where
vishva vidyālaya	University
pichhalē sāl	last year

bhī	also
naukarī	service
sarkārī	governmental, of the government
afsar	officer

Past Continuous

मैं जा रहा था	*maiñ jā rahā thā*	I was going.
मैं जा रही थी	*maiñ jā rahī thī*	I was going
हम जा रहे थे	*ham jā rahē thē*	We were go
तुम जा रहे थे	*tum jā rahē thē*	You were go
आप जा रहे थे	*āp jā rahē thē*	You were go
आप जा रही थीं	*āp jā rahī thīñ*	You were ing.
वह जा रहा था	*vah jā rahā thā*	He was going.
वह जा रही थी	*vah jā rahī thī*	She was going.
वे जा रहे थे	*vē jā rahē thē*	They were going.
वे जा रही थीं	*vē jā rahī thīñ*	They were going. (F)

Verbs in past continuous follows the same rule as in present continuous except that the auxiliary verb in the end is *tha, thi, thē* (was, were) instead of *hūñ, hai, haiñ* (am, is, are).

आप क्या कर रहे हैं ?	*āp kyā kar rahē haiñ?*	What are you doing?
मैं पत्र लिख रहा हूं।	*maiñ patra likh rahā hūñ*	I am writing a letter.
किसको पत्र लिख रहे हैं?	*kiskō patra likh rahē haiñ?*	To whom are you writing the letter?
मैं अपनी माँ को लिख रहा हूं	*maiñ apnī mā kō likh rahā hūñ*	I am writing to my mother.
आप पत्र हिन्दी मे लिख रहे हैं ?	*āp patra Hindi mē likh rahē haiñ?*	Are you writing the letter in Hindi?
जी हाँ, आज-कल मैं हिन्दी सीख रहा हूं।	*jī hāñ, āj-kal maiñ Hindi sīkh rahā hūñ*	Yes, these days I am learning Hindi.
और मैं हिन्दी पढ़ा रहा हूं।	*aur maiñ Hindi paṛhā rahā hūñ*	And I am teaching Hindi.

New Words

patra	letter
likhnā	to write
mā kō	to mother

apnī	my
hindı mē	in Hindi
āj-kal	these days
sīkhnā	to learn
parhānā	to teach
aur	and

Past Perfect

मैं गया था	*maiñ gayā thā*	I had gone.
मैं गयी थी	*maiñ gayi thī*	I had gone. (F)
हम गये थे	*ham gayē thē*	We had gone.
तुम गये थे	*tum gayē thē*	You had gone.
आप गये थे	*āp gayē thē*	You had gone.
आप गयी थीं	*āp gayı thīñ*	You had gone (F)
वह गया था	*vah gayā thā*	He had gone.
वह गयी थी	*vah gayī thı*	She had gone.
वे गये थे	*vē gayē thē*	They had gone.
वे गयी थीं	*vē gayı thīñ*	They had gone.(F)
आप आज दफतर गये थे?	*āp āj daftar gayē thē?*	Did you go to office today?
जी नही, आज मैं दफतर नहीं गया था	*jı nahiñ, āj maiñ daftar nahiñ gayā thā*	No, I did not go to office today.

मैं बाज़ार गया था	*maiñ bāzār gayā thā*	I had gone to the market.
मैं आपके घर गया था	*maiñ āpkē ghar gayā thā*	I went to your house.
कल शाम आप कहां गये थे ?	*kal shām āp kahāñ gayē thē?*	Where had you been yesterday?
कल बंबई से मेरा दोस्त आया था	*kal Bambai sē mērā dōst āyā thā*	Yesterday my friend had come from Bombay.
उसने मेरे साथ खाना खाया था	*usnē mērē sāth khānā khāyā thā*	He had meals with me yesterday.
मेरी पत्नी ने खाना पकाया था	*mēri patni nē khānā pakāyā thā*	My wife had coocked the meal.

Future Tense

(भविष्य *Bavishya*)

मैं जाऊंगा	*maiñ jāūngā*	I shall go. (M)
मैं जाऊंगी	*maiñ jāūngī*	I shall go. (F)
हम जाएंगे	*ham jāēngē*	We shall go.
तुम जाओगे	*tum jāōgē*	You shall go.

तुम जाओगी	*tum jāōgī*	You shall go. (F)
आप जाएंगे	*āp jāēngē*	You shall go.
आप जाएंगी	*āp jāēngī*	You shall go. (F)
वह जाएगा	*vah jāēgā*	He will go.
वह जाएगी	*vah jāēgī*	She will go. (F)
वे जाएंगे	*vē jāēngē*	They will go.
वे जाएंगी	*vē jāēngī*	They will go. (F)

To form the future tense, add to the verb root—

1st person:	ūngā	to masculine singular
	ūngī	to feminine singular
	ēngē	to masculine plural
	ēngī	to feminine plural
2nd person:	ōgē	masculine singular and plural (tum)
	ōgī	feminine singular and plural (tum)
	ēngē	masculine singular and plural (āp)
	ēngī	feminine singular and plural (āp)
3rd person:	ēgā	masculine singular
	ēngē	masculine plural

ēgī feminine singular
ēngī feminine plural

कल सवेरे आप घर पर होंगे ? *kal savērē āp ghar par hōngē*	Will you be at home tomorrow morning?
आप कितने बजे आना चाहेंगे ? *āp kitnē bajē ānā chāhēngē?*	At what o'clock would you like to come?
मैं आठ बजे आना चाहूंगा। *maiñ āṭh bajē ānā chā-hūngā*	I would like to come at eight o'clock.
आप नौ बजे आ सकेंगे ? *āp nau bajē ā sakēngē?*	Will you be able to come at nine o'clock?
जी हां, मैं नौ बजे आऊंगा। *jī hāñ maiñ nau bajē āūngā*	Yes, I shall come at nine o'clock.
मैं आपकी प्रतीक्षा करूंगा। *maiñ āpkī pratīkshā karūngā*	I shall wait for you.
मैं ठीक नौ बजे पहुंचूंगा। *maiñ ṭhīk nau bajē pahu-chūngā*	I shall reach exactly at nine o'clock.

धन्यवाद ! अब मैं जाऊंगा। *dhanyavād, ab maiñ jāungā*	Thank you! I shall go now.
आप चाय नहीं पिएंगे ? *āp chāe nahīñ piēngē?*	Will you not take tea?
जी नहीं, धन्यवाद। मैं सिर्फ ठंडा पानी पिऊंगा। *jī nahīñ, dhanyavād, maiñ sirf ṭhanḍā pānī piūngā*	No, thanks. I shall drink only cold water.
चाय में देर नहीं होगी। बिल्कुल तैयार है। *chāē mēñ dēr nahīñ hōgī, bilkul taiyār hai*	Tea will not take long. It is absolutely ready.
चाय के साथ कुछ खाएंगे ? *Chāe kē sāth kuchh khāēngē ?*	Will you have something to eat with tea?
जी नहीं, धन्यवाद। अब मैं चलूंगा। देर हो जाएगी। *jī nahīñ, dhanyavād. ab maiñ chalūngā. dēr hō jāēgī*	No, thanks. Now I shall make a move. It will be late.

New Words

savērē	in the morning
ghar par	at home

hoṅge	will be
kitne bajē	at what o' clock
chāhēngē	would like
ā skēngē?	can you come?
pratīkshā karnā	to wait
pratīkshā (n)	
piēngē	will drink
dēr	delay
taiyār	ready
kuchh	something
chalūngā	shall move on, shall go
hō jāyēgī	will happen

(In English the literal meaning of dēr hō jāegī would be 'delay will happen.')

Request or Command :

This form of the verb in English is known as the imperative mood. The following examples will make it clear how this is formed. It is formed differently in the case of *tum* or *āp*. In the case of *tum* it may be a command or a wish. In the case of *āp* it may be a wish or a request as this form is the polite form. It would be more polite if *kripayā* (please) is added in the beginning.

(तुम) दूध पिओ	(*tum*) *dūdh piō*	Drink milk.
(तुम) रोटी खाओ	(*tum*) *rōṭı khāō*	Eat bread.
गरम चाय लाओ	*garam chāe lāo*	Bring hot tea.
(आप) दूध पीजिए	*āp dūdh pījiyē*	Please drink milk
(आप) रोटी खाइए	*ap rōṭī khāiyē*	Please eat bread.
कृपया, अन्दर आइए	*kripayā andar āiyē*	Please come in.
कृपया, बैठिए	*kripayā, baiṭhiyē*	Please be seated.

In the case of negative imperative, forbidding a person from doing something, *mat* is added before the verb.

फूल मत तोड़ो	*phūl mat tōṛō*	Don't pluck flowers.
गाड़ी तेज़ मत चलाओ	*gāṛi ıēz mat cha.āō*	Don't drive the car fast.
कृपया जोर से मत बोलिए	*kripayā zōr sē mat bōliyē*	Please don't talk loudly.
कृपया आप बाहर प्रतीक्षा कीजिए	*kripayā āp bāhar pratıkshā kījiyē*	Please wait outside.

कृपया दरवाजा खोलिए	*kripayā darvāzā khōliyē*	Please open the door.
कृपया दरवाजा बंद कीजिए	*kripayā darvāzā band kījiyē*	Please close the door.
कृपया कल शाम मेरे साथ खाना खाइए	*kripayā kal shām mērē sāth khānā khāiyē*	Please have dinner with me tomorrow evening.
आप मेरे साथ चलिए	*āp mērē sāth chaliyē*	Came with me.
बाहर मत जाइए	*bāhar mat jāiyē*	Don't go out.
बच्चो, बारिश में मत खेलो	*bachchō, bārish mē mat khēlō*	Children, don't play in the rain.

Given below are some common verbs and their imperative form. Readers are advised to use them in sentences as an exercise.

आना	*ānā*	आओ, आइए	*ā-ō, āiyē*
जाना	*jānā*	जाओ, जाइए	*jāō, jāiyē*
खाना	*khānā*	खाओ, खाइए	*khāō, khaiyē*
देखना	*dēkhnā*	देखो, देखिए	*dēkhō, dēkhiyē*

लिखना	*likhnā*	लिखो, लिखिए	*likhō, likhiyē*
पढ़ना	*paṛhnā*	पढ़ो, पढ़िए	*paṛhō, paṛhiyē*
गाना	*gānā*	गाओ, गाइए	*gāō, gāiyē*
करना	*karnā*	करो, कीजिए	*karō, kariyē*
पीना	*pīnā*	पीओ, पीजिए	*pīō, pījiyē*
लेना	*lēnā*	लो, लीजिए	*lō, lījiyē*
बोलना	*bōlnā*	बोलो, बोलिए	*bōlō, bōliyē*
सुनना	*sunanā*	सुनो, सुनिए	*sunō, suniyē*

pījiyē, kījiyē, lījiyē and *dījiyē* are irregular as seen from the examples above.

Sometimes indefinite is used as imperative in second person (tum).

बाहर मत जाना	*bāhar mat jāna*	Don't go out.
एक गिलास पानी लाना	*ēk gilās pānī lānā*	Bring a glass of water.
खाना गरम करना	*khānā garam karnā*	Warm up the food.
फल काटना	*phal kāṭnā*	Cut the fruits.

Subjunctive Mood

When a verb is in a subjunctive mood, usually the sentence has two clauses; the verb in one of the clauses is in the subjunctive mood, that is, it lays down a condition, a wish or a purpose

मैंने उसको पैसे दिए जिससे वह खाना खा सके

māinē uskō paisē diyē jisasē vah khānā kha sakē

I gave him money so that he may eat food.

मैंने तुम्हारा वेतन बढ़ाया जिससे तुम ज्यादा अच्छा काम करो

māinē tumhara vētan baṛhāyā jisasē tum zyādā achchhā kām karō

I raised your pay so that you may work better.

मैंने आग जलाई जिससे कमरा गरम हो जाए

māinē āg jalāyī jisasē kamrā garam hō jaē

lit the fire so that the room becomes warm.

New Words

paisē	paise, money
jisasē	so that
khā sakē	can eat
vētan	pay
baṛhāyā	raised, increased
zyādā achchhā	better
karō	do
āg	fire

jalāyī	burnt
ho jāē	becomes

Another form of conditional verb :

अगर आप आएं तो मेरी किताब ले आएं। *agar āp ayēñ tō mērī kitāb lē ayēñ*	If you come, please bring my book.
अगर वह आए तो उसे मेरे पास भेज दें। *agar vah ayē to usē mērē pās bhēj dēñ*	If he comes, please send him to me.
अगर वह भूखा हो तो उसे रोटी दे दें। *agar vah bhūkhā hō tō usē rōṭī dē dēñ*	If he is hungry, give him bread.
अगर मेरे गुरु जी आएँ तो कमरे में बिठा देना। *agar mērē guruji ayēñ tō kamarē mēñ biṭha dēnā*	If my teacher comes make he sit in the room.

These sentences have doubt clauses too. The first clause express a doubt, if this happens, and the second clause gives an order or makes a request.

Interrogative Words

कौन	*kaun*	who
क्या	*kyā*	what

क्यों	*kyōñ*	why
कब	*kab*	when
कब तक	*kab tak*	until! when, by what time
कहां	*kahāñ*	where
कैसे	*kaisē*	how
कौन-सा	*kaun-sā*	which, which one
किसको	*kiskō*	who
किसका	*kiskā*	whose
कितने	*kitanē*	how many
कितना	*kitanā*	how much

It is interesting that all the interrogative words begin with *ka*. Now let us use them in sentences.

यह आदमी कौन है? — Who is this man?
yah ādamī kaun hai?

उसका नाम क्या है? — What is his name?
uskā nām kyā hai?

वह क्यों आया है? — Why has he come?
vah kyōñ āyā hai?

वह कब जाएगा? — When will he go?
vah kab jāyēgā?

वह कब तक रहेगा? *vah kab tak rahēgā?*	How long will he stay?
आप कहाँ जा रहे हैं? *āp kahāñ jā rahē haiñ?*	Where are you going?
आप कैसे हैं? *āp kaisē haiñ?*	How are you?
आपकी कलम कौन-सी है? *āpkī kalam kaun-sī hai?*	Which one is your pen?
आप यह किताब किसको देंगे? *āp yah kitāb kiskō dēngē?*	To whom will you giv this book?
यह किसका मकान है? *yah kiskā makān hai?*	Whose house is this?
आपके पास कितने रुपये हैं? *āpke pās kitanē rupayē? haiñ?*	How many rupees do you have?
आपको कितना आटा चाहिए *āpkō kitnā ātā chāhiē?*	How much flour do you want?
मुझको पानी चाहिए *mujhkō panī chāhiē*	I want water.
मुझको एक किलो आलू चाहिए *mujhkō ēk kilō ālū chāhiē*	I want a kilo of potatoes.

आपको क्या चाहिए? *āpkō kyā chāhiē?*	What do you want?
बच्चे को खिलौना चाहिए *bachchē kō khilaunā chāhiē*	The child wants a toy.
बच्चा भूखा है, उसको दूध चाहिए *bachchā bhūkhā hai, uskō dūdh chāhiē*	The child is hungry, he wants milk.
उसको यह कपड़ा दो मीटर चाहिए *uskō yeh kapṛa dō mītar chāhiē*	He wants two metres of this cloth.

Chāhiē is a word you are likely to use very often. It is important to note the construction of a sentence with *chāhiē* which means needed or wanted. Literally translated into English it would mean wanted or needed to me e.g. one kilo of potatoes is needed to me!

Can, Could

सकना *sakanā* (to be able to)

Present Tense

आप हिन्दी बोल सकते हैं? *āp Hindi bol sakatē haiñ?*	Can you speak Hindi ?

जी हाँ, मैं कुछ-कुछ बोल सकता हूं। *jī hāñ, maiñ kuchh-kuchh bōl sakatā hūñ*	Yes I can speak a little.
लेकिन, मैं अच्छी तरह समझ सकता हूं। *lēkin, maiñ ahhchhī tarah samajh sakatā hūñ*	But, I can understand well.
आप पढ़ भी सकते हैं? *āp paṛh bhī sakatē haiñ?*	Can you also read?
जी नहीं, मैं पढ़ या लिख नहीं सकता। *jī nahīñ, maiñ paṛh yā likh nahiñ sakatā.*	No, I can not read or write.

Future Tense

आप आज शाम मेरे घर आ सकेंगे? *āp āj shām mērē ghar ā sakēngē?*	Will you be able to come to my house this evening?
मुझको अफसोस है, मैं नहीं आ सकूंगा।	I am sorry, I shall not be able to come.

mujhkō afsōs hai,
maiñ nahiñ ā sakūngā

आप अभी पाँच मिनट में तैयार हो सकेंगे ? *āp abhī panch minat mēñ taiyār hō sakēngē?*	Can you get ready now within five minutes?
आप गा सकते हैं ? *āp gā sakatē haiñ?*	Can you sing?
मैं सिर्फ बंगाली गीत गा सकता हूं। *maiñ sirf Bengālī gīt gā sakatā hūñ*	I can sing only Bengali songs.

Past Tense

मैं जा सकता था, लेकिन गया नहीं *maiñ jā sakatā thā, lēkin gayā nahiñ*	I could have gone, but I did not go.
मैं नहीं जा सका । *maiñ nahiñ jā sakā*	I could not go.
मैं नहीं देख सका *maiñ nahīñ dēkh sakā*	I was not able to see.

माफ कीजिए, मैं कल नहीं आ सका। *māf kījiyē, maiñ kal nahiñ ā sakā*	Forgive me, I could not come yesterday.

Another interesting variation in Hindi is in the verb, to like *pasand karnā*. It is formed by two words. Usually it is used in a passive manner of speech. For example, I like mangoes would be *mujhkō ām pasand haiñ.*

मुझको नाचना पसंद है *mujhkō nāchanā pasand hai*	I like to dance.
मुझको दिल्ली पसंद है *mujhkō Dillī pasand hai*	I like Delhi.
आपको कौन-सा फल सब से ज्यादा पसन्द है ? *āpkō kaun-sā phal sab sē zyādā pasand hai?*	Which fruit do you like the most?
मुझको सेब सबसे ज्यादा पसंद है *mujhkō sēb sabsē zyādā pasand hai*	I like apples the most (more than all others).

आपको मसालेदार खाना पसंद है ?	Do you like spicy food?
āpkō masālēdār khānā pasand hai?	
मुझको ज्यादा मसाला पसंद नहीं है	I do not like too much spices.
mujhkō zyādā masālā pasand nahīñ hai	

New Words

bōl	to speak
kuchh-kuchh	a little, somewhat
samajh	understand
achchhī tarah	well, properly
paṛh	read
likh	write
afsōs	regret
taiyār	ready
hōnā	to be
gā	sing
gīt	song
lēkin	but
māf kījiyē	excuse me
nachanā	to dance
sēb	apple
masālēdār	spicy

Transitive And Intransitive Verbs

	Intransitive			*Transitive*	
सोना	*sōnā*	to sleep	सुलाना	*sulānā*	to put to sleep
हंसना	*hansnā*	to laugh	हंसाना	*hansānā*	to make others laugh
रोना	*rōnā*	to weep	रुलाना	*rulānā*	to make someone weep
खेलना	*khēlanā*	to play	खेलाना	*khelānā*	to make someone play
उठना	*uṭhanā*	to get up	उठाना	*uṭhānā*	to make someone get up, or to wake up someone
जीना	*jīnā*	to live	जिलाना	*jilānā*	to give life to someone
कटना	*kaṭanā*	to cut	काटना	*kāṭanā*	to cut

नाचना	*nāchanā*	to dance	नचाना	*nachānā*	to make some-one dance
मरना	*marnā*	to die	मारना	*mārnā*	to kill
पिटना	*piṭanā*	to be beaten up	पीटना	*piṭanā*	to beat
डरना	*darnā*	to fear	डराना	*darāna*	to frighten
चिढ़ना	*chirhṇā*	to be teased	चिढ़ाना	*chiṛhānā*	to tease

Examples:

मैं डर गया	*maiñ ḍar gayā*	I was frightened
मैंने उसको डरा दिया	*mainē usakō ḍarā ḍiyā*	I frightened him
मैं हंसा	*maiñ hansā*	I laughed.
मैंने उसको हंसाया	*mainē usakō nansāyā*	I made him laugh.
मैं खेल रहा हूं	*maiñ khēl rahā hūñ*	I am playing.

मैं बच्चों को खेला रहा हूं	*maiñ bachchōñ kō khelā rahā hūñ*	I am making the children play.
मैं सो रहा था	*maiñ sō rahā thā*	I was sleeping.
मैं बच्चे को सुला रहा था	*maiñ bachchē kō sulā rahā thā*	I was putting the child to sleep.
तुम क्यों रो रहे हो ?	*tum kyōñ rō rahē hō?*	Why are you crying ?
तुम उसे क्यों रुला रहे हो ?	*tum usē kyōñ rulā rahē hō?*	Why are you making him cry?
वह मुझको चिढ़ाता है।	*vah mujhakō chiṛhātā hai*	He teases me.

Transitive			Causative		
करना	*karnā*	to do	करवाना	*karavāna*	to make someone do
पीना	*pīnā*	to drink	पिलवाना	*pilavānā*	to make someone drink
खाना	*khānā*	to eat	खिलाना	*khilānā*	to feed

सुनना	*sunanā*	to hear	सुनाना	*sunānā*	to narrate
देखना	*dēkhanā*	to see	दिखाना	*dikhānā*	to show
सीना	*sīnā*	to sew	सिलाना	*silānā*	to get someone to sew
पकाना	*pakānā*	to cook	पकवाना	*pakavānā*	to get cooked
मारना	*mārnā*	to beat	मरवाना	*marvānā*	to get someone to beat

Examples

मैंने काम किया	*mainē kām kiyā*	I did work.
मैंने काम करवाया	*mainē kām karvāyā*	I got the work done.
मैंने रोटी खाई	*mainē rōti khāyi*	I ate bread.
मैंने उसको रोटी खिलवाई	*mainē usakō rōti khilavāyī*	I fed him bread .
मैंने एक कहानी सुनी	*mainē ēk kahāni sunī*	I heard a story.
मैंने उसको कहानी सुनवाई	*mainē usakō kahani sunvāyi*	I narrated him a story.
मैंने तस्वीर देखी	*mainē tasvīr dekhi*	I saw the picture.
मैंने तस्वीर दिखाई	*mainē tasvīr dikhāyi*	I showed the picture.
मैंने उसको मारा	*mainē usakō mārā*	I beat him.
मैंने उसको मरवाया	*mainē usakō marvāyā*	I got him beaten up.

CHAPTER EIGHT

ADVERBS

(क्रिया विशेषण *Kriya Visheshan*)

चाय बहुत गरम है *chāe ahut garam hai*	Tea is very hot.
वह तेज चलता है *vah tēz chaltā hai*	He walks fast.
मुझको बिल्कुल नहीं मालूम *mujhkō bilkul nahīñ mālūm*	It is not known to me at all.
मैं वहां जा रहा हूं *maīñ vahāñ jā rahā hūñ*	I am going there.
वह काफ़ी दूर चला गया *vah kāfī dūr chalā gayā*	He has gone quite far away.
वह फौरन आ गया *vah fauran ā gayā*	He came immediately.

In Hindi an adverb precedes the verb or adjective it qualifies as seen in the examples given above.

Sometimes an adverb is repeated to emphasise and also for effectiveness of speech.

जल्दी-जल्दी काम करो *jaldi-jaldi kām karō*	Work fast.
धीरे-धीरे खाओ *dhīrē-dhīrē khāō*	Eat slowly.
धीरे-धीरे बोलिए *dhīrē-dhīrē bōliyē*	Speak slowly.
आप कहाँ-कहाँ जाएँगे? *āp kahāñ-kahāñ jāengē?*	Which are the places you will go to? (When more than one place is indicated)
वह कब-कब आता है? *vah kab-kab ātā hai?*	When does he come? (What are the days or time when he comes?)

Another thing to remember is that where words like above (üpar) or below (nīchē) are used they are preceded by a preposition.

Examples:

मेज के ऊपर *mēz kē ūpar*	on the table.
मेज के नीचे *mēz kē nīchē*	under the table.

घर के चारों ओर *ghar kē chārōñ ōr*	around the house—or all the four sides of the house.
नदी के पार *nadī kē pār*	beyond the river.
नदी के उस पार *nadī kē us pār*	on the other side of the river.
नदी के किनारे *nadī kē kinārē*	on the river side.
जमीन के नीचे *zamīn kē nīchē*	under the ground.
घर के पास *ghar kē pās*	near the house.
घर से दूर *ghar sē dūr*	far from the house.
उसके बारें में *uskē bārē mēñ*	about him.
घर के सामने *ghar kē sāmnē*	in front of the house.
घर के पीछे *ghar kē pīchhē*	behind the house.

दो घरों के बीच में *dō gharōñ kē bīch mēñ*	between two houses.
शहर के बीचो बीच *shahar kē bichōbīch*	right in the centre of the town.
बाग के ठीक बीच में *bāg kē thīk bīch mēñ*	right in the centre of the garden.
वे साथ-साथ गए *vē sāth-sāth gayē*	They went together.
वे अलग-अलग गए *ve alag-alag gayē*	They went separately.
एक साथ गए *ek-sāth gayē*	Went together.
घर के आस-पास दुकानें हैं *ghar kē ās-pās dūkānēñ haiñ*	There are shops near-about the house.

Reading Exercise

आपके घर के सामने कौन रहता है? *āpkē ghar kē sāmanē kaun rahatā hai?*	Who lives in front of your house?
मेरे बाग के बीचो बीच फव्वारा है	There is a fountain right in the centre of

mērē bāg kē bichōñbīch phavvārā hai	my garden.
मेरा कमरा अलग है *mērā kamarā alag hai*	My room is separate.
मेरे घर के पास बाजार है *mērē ghar kē pās bāzār hai*	There is a market near my house.
मेरे घर के आस-पास कई दुकानें हैं *mērē ghar kē ās-pās kaī dukanēñ haiñ*	There are several shops near about my house.
आपके घर के ऊपर कौन रहता है? *āpkē ghar kē ūpar kaun rahtā hai*	Who lives above your house?
आपकी मेज़ के नीचे बिल्ली है *āpkī mēz kē nīchē billī hai*	There is a cat under your table.
घरों के बीच में बाग है *gharōñ kē bīch mēñ bāg hai*	There is a garden in between the houses.

राम और सीता साथ-साथ स्कूल गए *Rām aur Sītā sāth-sāth skūl gayē*	Ram and Sita went to school together.
इन चीज़ों को एक साथ मत रखो *in chīzōñ kō ēk sāth mat rakhō*	Don't keep these things together.
नदी के उस पार जंगल है *nadī kē us pār jangal hai*	There is a forest on the other side of the river.
मेरा घर नदी के किनारे है *mērā ghar nadī kē kinārē hai*	My house is by the side of the river.
मेरा दफ्तर घर से दूर है *mērā daftar ghar sē dūr hai.*	My office is far away from the house.
मेरा घर स्कूल के पास है *mērā ghar skūl kē pās hai*	My house is near the school.
मेरा घर स्कूल से ज्यादा दूर	My house is not very

नहीं है *mērā ghar skūl se zyādā dūr nahīñ hai*	far from the school.
मेरे घर के चारों ओर आम के पेड हैं *mērē ghar kē chārōñ ōr ām kē pēṛ haiñ*	There are mango trees all around my house.

Telling the Time

कितने बजे हैं? *kitanē bajē haiñ?*	What time is it?
क्या वक्त है? *kyā vakt hai?*	What is the time?
क्या समय है? *kyā samya hai?*	What is the time?
एक बजा है *ek bajā hai*	It is one o'clock.
डेढ़ बजे हैं *dērh bajē haiñ*	It is half past one.
दो बजे हैं *dō bajē haiñ*	It is two o'clock.

ढाई बजे हैं *ḍhāī bajē haiñ*	It is half past two.
तीन बजे हैं *tīn bajē haīñ*	It is three o'clock.
सवा तीन बजे हैं *savā tīn bājē haīñ*	It is a quarter past three.
साढ़े चार बजे हैं *sarḥē chār bajē haiñ*	It is half past four.
पौने पांच बजे हैं *paunē pānch bajē haīñ*	It is a quarter to five.

Note that a quarter is *savā.* 'Half past' or half in respect of time, weight or measurement is *sarḥē*, *paune* is three fourths or three quarters. Three and a half metre will be *sarḥē tīn mīṭar*, three and three-fourth metre will be *paunē chār mīṭar,* four and a quarter metre will be *savā mītar* and so on.

Please also note that one and a half is not *sarhē ēk* but *dērḥ*, similarly two and a half is not *sarḥē do* but *ḍhā-ī.*

तीन बजने को पाँच मिनट हैं *tīn bajanē kō pānch*	It is five minutes to

minat haiñ	three.
तीन बज कर दस मिनट *tīn baj kar das minat*	It is ten minutes past three.
ठीक बारह् बजे हैं *thīk bārah bajē haiñ*	It is exactly twelve o'clock.
मेरा दफ्तर दस बजे से पाँच बजे तक होता है *mērā daftar das bajē sē pānch bajē tak hōtā hai*	My office is from ten o'clock to five o'clock
मेरी घड़ी पांच मिनट तेज है *mērī ghaṛi pānch minat tez hai*	My watch is fast by five minutes.
मेरी घड़ी आगे है *mērī ghaṛī āgē hai*	My watch is fast.
मेरी घड़ी पाँच मिनट पीछे है *mērī ghaṛi pānch minat pīchhē hai*	My watch is slow by five minutes.
मेरी घड़ी बन्द है *mērī ghaṛī band hai*	My watch is closed. (literal meaning)

मेरी घड़ी रुक गई है *mērī gharī ruk gayī hai*	My watch has stopped.
आपकी घड़ी ठीक है? *āpkī gharī thik hai?*	Is your watch correct?
मेरी घड़ी खराब है *mērī gharī kharāb hai.*	My watch is bad i.e. it is not working.
मेरी घड़ी चल नहीं रही है *mērī gharī chal nahīñ rahī hai*	My watch is not working.

New words

kitanē	how many

(*kitanē bajē haiñ?*—literally means—how many (hours) have struck?)

vakt, samay (M)	time
savā	quarter
dērh	o e and a half
ḍhāī	two and half
paunē	three quarters

(paune panch would mean three quarters of five)

ghaṛī (F)	watch
pīchhē	behind
āgē	ahead
rukanā	to stop
chalanā	to move
gharīsaz	watchmaker

Some common idioms

लगा *lagā*

वह बोलने लगा He began speaking.
vah bōlnē lagā

Although it would be quite grammatical and correct to se *usnē bōlnā shūrū kiyā* (he started speaking) but it is more idiomatic to say *vah bōlnē lagā*. It would not be possible to translate this idiom into English as there is nothing equivalent. It would be helpful to understand in what different meanings the word *lagā* can be used, and then to try and use them. When learning a language, one should always try and use the idioms in that language though it may be difficult to translate them into one's own mother tongue.

मेरा बच्चा अब चलने लगा है My child has now

mērā bachchā ab chalnē lagā hai	started walking.
जैसे ही मैं घर से निकला, बारिश होने लगी *jaisē hī maiñ ghar sē nikalā, bārish hōnē lagī*	As soon as I came out of the house, it started raining.
आपका बच्चा बोलने लगा? *āpakā bachchā bōlnē lagā?*	Has your child started speaking?
मेरा बच्चा चलने लगा है *mērā bachchā chalnē lagā hai*	My child has started walking.
बारिश होने लगी *bārish hōnē lagī*	It has started raining.

When '*laganā*' is used as the principal verb, it means it 'appears' or it feels'.

Examples:

मुझको ठंड लगती है *mujhkō ṭhanḍ lagatī hai*	I feel cold.
उसको भूख लग रही है *uskō bhūkh lag rahī hai*	He is feeling hungry.
बच्चे को प्यास लग रही है	The child is feeling

bachchē kō pyās lag rahī hai	thirsty.
मुझको नींद लग रही है *mujhko nīnd lag rahī hai*	I am feeling sleepy.
मुझको लगता है कि वह नहीं आएगा *mujhkō lagatā hai ki vah nahī ayēgā*	I feel he won't come.
मुझको लगता है मेरा पत्र आज जरूर आएगा *mujhkō lagatā hai mērā patra āj zarūr āyēgā*	I feel my letter will definitely come today.
मुझको बरसात अच्छी नहीं लगती *mujhkō barsāt achchhī nahīñ lagatī*	I do not like the rainy season.
आपको चाय ज्यादा अच्छी लगती है या काफी? *āpkō chāe zyādā achchhī lagatī hai yā kaufī?*	Which do you like better--tea or coffee?

मुझको बाग में काम करना अच्छा लगता है *mujhkō bāg mēñ kām karnā achchhā lagatā hai*	I like to work in the garden.
गीता सुन्दर लग रही है *gītā sundar lag rahī hai.*	Gita is looking pretty.
यह आदमी गरीब लगता है *yah ādamī garīb lagatā hai*	This man appears to be poor.
यह आदमी चालाक लगता है *yah ādamī chālāk lagatā hai*	This man appears to be cunning.
लगता है वह सो गया *lagata hai vah so gayā*	It appears that he has gone to sleep.
लगता है वह चला गया *lagatā hai vah chalā gayā*	It appears that he has left.
लगता है वह खा चुका *lagtā hai vah khā chukā*	It appears that he has already eaten.

लगता है उसने पत्र नहीं पढा — It appears he has not read the letter.
lagatā hai usnē patra nahīñ parḥā

Note :—It should be noted that when a sentence is negative, i.e., it has the word **nahīñ**, the auxiliary verb is often dropped.

Two verbs are often used together. For example

मैं जाना चाहता हूँ — I wish to go.
maiñ jānā chahtā hūñ

वह क्या खाना चाहता है? — What does he wish to eat?
vah kyā khānā chāhtā hai?

When '*lagā*' is used with another verb, like *mērā bachchā chalnē lagā*, the first verb is invariably in the form *chalnē*, *khānē*, *sonē*, *pinē*, etc., irrespective of the gender, person or number of the subject, noun or pronoun. It is the verb *lagā* which changes according to the subject.

Example:

Present—

maiñ............*lagatā hūñ*
maiñ............*lagatī hūñ*
ham............*lagatē haiñ*

vah..........*lagatā hai* and so on.

Future—

maiñ	*lagūngā, lagūngī*
ham	*lagēngē*
vah	*lagēgā, lagēgī*
ve	*lagēngē*
tum	*lagōgē*
āp	*lagēngē, lagēngī*

Examples

मैं कल से दफ्तर जाने लगूँगा *maiñ kal sē daftar jānē lagūngā*	I shall start going to the office from tomorrow.
वह कल से काम करने लगेगा *vah kal sē kām karnē lagēgā*	He will start working from tomorrow.
आप कब से स्कूल जाने लगेंगी? *āp kab sē skūl jānē lagēngī?*	When will you start going to the school?
अन्दर बैठिए, बाहर ठंड	Si inside, it will be

लगेगी — cold outside.

andar baithiyē, bāhar ṭhanḍ lagēgī

रोटी खाइए, नहीं तो भूख लगेगी — Eat bread, otherwise you will feel hungry.

rōṭī khāiyē, nahīn tō bhūkh lagēgī

Past Tense

आपको ठंड लगी? — Did you feel cold?

āpkō ṭhanḍ lagī?

आपको यह शहर अच्छा लगा? — Did you like this city?

āpkō yah shahar achchhā lagā?

वे कब से काम पर जाने लगे? — When did they start going to work?

ve kab sē kām par jānē lagē?

Chāhnā means to wish or to want. If it is used by itself, like:

राम सीता को चाहता है

Ram Sita kō chahtā hai

It means Ram is fond of Sita. Or, *māīñ apnī billī kō bahut chāhtī hūñ,* (I love my cat very much). But when it is combined with another verb as given above, it means to want or to wish. The first verb is always used in the infinitive form—*jānā, ānā, gānā,* and so on. It is the second verb *chāhtā* which will keep changing the form to agree with the number, gender or the person of the subject.

Example

मैं चाय पीना चाहता हूं । *maiñ chāe pīnā chāhtā hūñ*	I want to drink tea.
मैं आपका गाना सुनना चाहती हूं । *maiñ āpkā gānā sunanā chāhtī hūñ*	I want to hear you sing.
वह मेरे घर आना चाहता है। *vah mērē ghar ānā chāhtā hai*	He wants to come to my house.
बच्चे बाहर खेलना चाहते हैं। *bachchē bāhar khēlanā chāhtē haiñ*	Children want to play outside.

चुकना
Chukanā

Chukanā means to finish. It is added to a verb to mean finishing a job or the end of something.

मैं खा चुका *maiñ khā chukā*	I have finished my meal
मैं चाय पी चुका *maiñ chāe pī chukā*	I have already had tea.
मैं यह फिल्म देख चुका *maiñ yeh film dēkh chukā*	I have already seen this film.
वह काम कर चुका? *vah kām kar chukā?*	Has he finished the job?
आप खाना पका चुके? *āp khānā pakā chukē?*	Have you finished cooking?

The word *chukā* may also be used with an adjective, but in that case it is usually combined with *hō* (to be) the verb complete.

Example

काम खतम हो चुका? *kām khatam hō chukā?*	Has the work been completed?
खाना ठंडा हो चुका *khānā ṭhanḍā hō chukā*	The food has become cold.
जब मैं खाने बैठी, खाना ठंडा	When I sat down to

हो चुका था *jab maiñ khānē baiṭhī, khānā ṭhanḍā hō chukā thā*	eat, the food had already turned cold.
जब मैं चली तो बारिश खतम हो चुकी थी *jab maiñ chalī tō bārish khatam hō chukī thī*	When I started, the rain had already stopped.
जब मैं आया तो वह जा चुके थे *jab maiñ āyā tō vah jā chukē thē*	When I came he had already left.

'Chukā' adds the sense of finality to the meaning.

Future Tense

वह जा चुके होंगे *vah jā chukē hōngē*	He will have gone or he must have gone.
वह खा चुकी होगी *vah khā chukī hōngī*	She will have finished her meal.
काम खतम हो गया होगा	The work will have

kām khatam hō gayā hōgā	been finished.
वह किताब पढ़ चुका होगा *vah kitāb paṛh chukā hōgā*	He will have finished reading the book.
कल इस समय तक मैं जा चुकी होऊँगी *kal is samaya tak maiñ jā chukī hōungī*	Tomorrow by this time I will have gone.
मैंने सोचा आप खाना खा चुके होंगे *mainē sōchā āp khānā khā chukē hōnge*	I thought you must have finished eating.
मैंने सोचा आप यह किताब पढ़ चुके होंगे *mainē sōchā āp yah kitāb paṛh chukē hōngē*	I thought you must have read this book.

The use of ही *hī*, and तो *tō*

Hī **is often used to emphasise a word in, its exclusiveness.**

For example

सिर्फ आप ही अन्दर आ Only you can

सकते हैं *sirf āp hī andar ā sakatē haiñ*	come in.
मैं सिर्फ रोटी ही खाऊंगा' *maiñ sirf rōṭī hī khāūngā*	ɪ shall eat only bread.
आप आज काम ही करते रहेंगे, खाना नहीं खाएगें? *āp āj kām hī karatē rahēngē, khānā nahīñ khayēngē?*	Today you will only keep wòrking, will you not eat?

tō is sometimes used to mean then, or after, and sometimes it is used only for emphasis. It has no equivalent in English. Example: when it means then or if,

आप जाएंगें तो मैं भी आऊंगा *āp jāyēngē tō maiñ bhī jāūngā*	If you go I shall go too.
वह आएगा तो उसको किताब दे देना *vah āyegā tō usakō kitāb dē dēnā*	When he comes (then) give him the book.

अगर वह मांगे तो उसको दूध दे देना *agar vah māngē tō uskō dūdh dē dēnā*.	If he asks, (then) give him milk.
आप खा चुकें तो यहाँ आइएगा *āp khā chukēñ tō yahāñ āiyēgā*	When you finish eating, (then) please come here. (Come when you have finished eating).
वह बुलाए तो जाना *vah bulāē tō jānā*	If he calls you (then) go. (Go if he calls you).
वह पैसे दे तो मत लेना *vah paisē dē tō mat lēnā*.	If he gives money, don't take it.

In the last two sentences given above, the infinitive form of the verb, *jānā* and *lēnā* is used as imperative. It has already been mentioned earlier in the chapter on verbs, that infinitive can be used as imperative with *tum*.

to is used here in the conditional form of the verb.

Although not mentioned, *agar* (if) is implied.

tō is also used to mean a different type of emphasis.

मैं तो नहीं जाऊंगा	I will not go.
maiñ tō nahīñ jāūngā	
यह काम तो मैं नहीं करूंगा	I will not do this job.
yah kām tō maiñ nahīñ karūngā	
रोटी तो मैं नहीं खाऊंगा	I will not eat bread
rōṭī tō maiñ nahīñ khāungā	

In the first sentence the emphasis is on *maiñ*, meaning whoever might go I shall not go. In the second sentence the emphasis is on *kām*, meaning whatever I do; I shall not do, this particular work. In the sentence the emphasis on *rōṭī* meaning I shall eat anything else, but not *rōṭī*.

Changing verbs in to Present Perfect or Past Perfect.

If the root of a verb end in ā or any other vowel, add yā, yī, or yē to it to form the present perfect or past perfect.

Example

जा	*jā*	will be		*gayā*]
आ	*ā*	will be	आया	*āyā*

खा	*khā*	will be	खाया	*khāyā*
पी	*pī*	will be	पिया	*piyā*
सो	*sō*	will be	सोया	*sōyā*

When the root of the verb ends in a consonant, the symbol of a (ा) is added to it,

Example

लग	*lag*	will be	लगा	*lagā*
काट	*kāṭ*	will be	काटा	*kāṭā*
देख	*dēkh*	will be	देखा	*dēkhā*
सुन	*sun*	will be	सुना	*sunā*

Reading Exercise I

राम—नमस्ते । आप कैसी हैं?

Ram—*namastē. āp kaisī haiñ?*

सीता—मैं ठीक हूं, धन्यवाद । और आप कैसे हैं?

Sita—*maiñ thīk hūñ. dhanyavād. aur āp kaisē haiñ?*

राम—मैं भी ठीक हूं । आपके पति कहां हैं?

Ram—*maiñ bhī ṭhīk hūñ. āpkē pati kahāñ haiñ?*

सीता—मेरे पति आगरा में हैं ।

Sita—*mērē pati āgarā mēñ haiñ.*

राम—आपका घर कहां है?

Ram—*āpkā ghar kahāñ hai?*

सीता—मेरा घर हौजखास में है ।

Sita—*mērā ghar Hauz Khās mēñ hai.*

राम—आपके कितने बच्चे हैं?

Ram—*āpkē kitanē bachchē haiñ?*

सीता—मेरे चार बच्चे हैं—दो बेटे और दो बेटियां ।

Sita—*mērē chār bachchē haiñ—dō bēṭē aur dō bēṭiyāñ.*

राम—बच्चों के नाम क्या हैं?

Ram—*bachchōñ kē nām kyā haiñ?*

सीता—लड़कों के नाम लव और कुश हैं ।

Sita—*laṛkōñ kē nām Lav aur Kush haiñ.*

राम—और लडकियों के नाम?

Ram—*aur laṛkiyōñ kē nām?*

सीता—लड़कियों के नाम गीता और रीता हैं ।

Sita—*laṛkiyōñ kē nām Gita aur Rita haiñ.*

राम—बहुत सुन्दर नाम हैं । आपका घर बड़ा है?

Ram—*bahut sundar nām haiñ. āpkā ghar baṛā hai?*

सीता—घर छोटा है, लेकिन बाग बड़ा है ।

Sita—*ghar chhaṭā hai; lēkin bāg baṛā hai.*

राम—कितने कमरे हैं?

Ram—*kitanē kamarē haiñ?*

सीता—चार कमरे हैं, एक बैठने-खाने का कमरा, और तीन

सोने के कमरे।

Sita—*chār kamarēñ haiñ. ēk baithanē-khānē kā kamarā, aur tīn sōnē kē kamarē.*

राम—आप चाय लेंगी या कुछ ठंडा?

Ram—*āp chāe lēngī yā kuchchh thaṇḍā?*

सीता—सिर्फ़ ठंडा पानी चाहिए।

Sita—*sirf thaṇḍā pānī chāhiyē.*

राम—आप फल खाइए। केले बहुत मीठे हैं।

Ram—*āp phal khāiye. kēlē bahut mīṭhē haiñ.*

सीता—आपकी पत्नी और बच्चे कहाँ हैं?

Sita—*āpkī patnī aur bachchē kahāñ haiñ?*

राम—बच्चे स्कूल में हैं। पत्नी रसोई में है।

Ram—*bachchē skūl mēñ haiñ. patnī rasōī mēñ hai.*

English translation of the text

Ram—Namaste. How are you?

Sita—I am all right, thank you, and how are you?

Ram—I am all right too. Where is your husband?

Sita—My husbanb is in Agra.

Ram—Where is your house?

Sita—My house is in Hauz Khas.

Ram—How many children have you?

Sita—I have four children—two sons and two daughters.

Ram—What are the children's names?

Sita—Boy's names are Lav and Kush.

Ram—And the girls names?

Sita—Girls names are Gita and Rita.

Ram—Names are very pretty. Is your house big?

Sita—The house is small, but the garden is big.

Ram—How many rooms are there?

Sita—There are four rooms. One sitting-dining room, and three bed-rooms.

Ram—Will you have tea or something cold?

Sita—I want only cold water.

Ram—Please eat the fruit. The bananas are very sweet.

Sita—Where are your wife and children?

Ram—Children are in the school, wife is in the kitchen.

New words

kaisī	how
dhanyavād	thank you
āpkē	your
patī	husband
mēñ	in
kitanē	how many
chār	four
dō	two
kyā	what
baiṭhanē-khānē kā kamarā	Sitting-dining roc
sonē kā kamarā	bedroom
chāe	tea
kuchh	some, something
ṭhanḍā	cold
sirf	only
chāhiye	need, want
khāiye	please eat
miṭhē	sweet
patnī	wife
skūl	school
rasōī	kitchen

*It would be noticed that *pati* and *patni*, though third person singular, have been treated as plural. As will be explained in detail in the chapter on verbs, in the second or third person singular, the plural form is used for politeness.

**Mērē chār bachchē haiñ* means, I have four children. Translated literally it would mean *mine four children are*. Translating literally explains how a sentence is constructed in Hindi. Since forms of expression vary from language to language, a literal translation from English into Hindi may become a bizzare expression in Hindi or vice versa. It is important, therefore, to know the form of expressions that are peculiar to the language you are learning. Otherwise you may be able to make yourself under- stood all right but you will not be speaking correct language.

*Also note the sentence *mujhko ṭhandā pānī chāhiyē*. (I want cold water). Translated literally it would be *mai ṭhandā pānī chahatā hūñ*, but the passive form is more common. Translated literally it would mean *to me cold water is needed*.

Reading Exercise II

भारत बहुत बड़ा देश है । यह बहुत प्राचीन देश है ।

Bhārat bahut baṛā dēsh hai. yah bahut prāchīn dēsh hai.

इसके उतर में हिमालय पहाड़ है । दक्षिण में हिंद महासागर है ।

isakē uttar mē Himālaya pahāṛ hai. dakshiṇ mēñ Hind Mahāsāgar hai.

पूर्व में बंगाल की खाड़ी है । पश्चिम में अरब महासागर है ।

purva mēñ bangal kī khāṛī hai. pashchim mēñ arab mahāsāgar hai.

गंगा सबसे बड़ी और पवित्र नदी है ।

gangā sabsē baṛī aur pavitra nadī hai.

भारत में कई बड़ी नदियां हैं ।

Bhārat mē kaī baṛī nadiyāñ haiñ.

भारत की राजधानी दिल्ली है ।

Bhārat kī rājdhānī Dillī hai.

दिल्ली सुन्दर नगर है ।

Dillī sundar nagar hai.

दूसरे बड़े नगर बंबई, कलकता, और मद्रास हैं ।

dūsarē baṛē nagar Bambai, Kalkattā aur Madrās haiñ.

भारत की आबादी बहुत ज्यादा है ।

Bhārat kī ābādī bahut zyādā hai.

Translation into English

India (Bharat) is a very big country. It is an ancient country. In the north are the Himalaya mountain ranges. In the South is the Indian Ocean. In the east is the Bay of Bengal. In the west is the Arabian Sea. Ganges is the biggest and the holiest river. There are several big rivers in India. Delhi is the capital of India. Delhi is a beautiful city. Other big cities are Bombay, Calcutta and Madras. There is over population in India.

New words

bahut	very
dēsh	country
prāchīm	ancient
uttar	north
pahāṛ	mountains
dakshiṇ	south
pūrva	east
pashchim	west
pavitra	holy
nadī	river

kaī	several
rājdhānī	capital
nagar	city
dusarē	others
ābādī	population
bahut zyādā	very much, too much.

Reading exercise III

मैं नई दिल्ली में रहता हूं। मेरा भाई पुरानी दिल्ली में रहता है। मेरी बहिन बम्बई में है। वह साल में एक बार दिल्ली आती है। उसके पति और बच्चे भी आते हैं। मेरा दफ्तर पुरानी दिल्ली में है। मैं हर रोज़ बस से आता-जाता हूं। हम लोग बंगाली हैं। मेरे माता-पिता कलकत्ता में रहते हैं। आपने कलकत्ता देखा है? मुझको कलकत्ता बहुत पसंद है। मुझको दिल्ली भी पसंद है। आप दक्षिण के हैं? आपकी पत्नी हिन्दी बोलती है? मेरी पत्नी हिन्दी कुछ-कुछ बोलती है। मेरे बच्चे अच्छी हिन्दी बोलते हैं। आप लोग बंगला समझते हैं?

maiñ Nai Dillī mēñ rahtā hūñ. mērā bhāī purānī Dillī mēñ rahtā hai. mērī bahīn Bambaī mēñ hai. vah sāl mēñ ēk bār Dillī ātī hai. Usakē pati aur bachche bhī āte haiñ. mera daftar purānī Dillī mēñ hai. maiñ har rōz bas sē ātā-jātā hūñ. ham lōg Bengāli haiñ.

mērē matā-pitā Kalakattā mēñ rahtē haiñ. āpnē Kalakattā dēkhā hai? mujhakō Kalakattā bahut pasand hai. mujhakō Dillī bhī pasand hai āp dakshiṇ kē haiñ? āpkī patnī hindī bōltī hai? mērī patnī hindī kuchh-kuchh bōlatī hai. mērē bachchē achchhi hindī bōlatē haiñ. āp lōg Banglā samajhatē haiñ?

I live in New Delhi. My brother lives in old Delhi. My sister lives in Bombay. She comes to Delhi once in the year. Her husband and children come too. My office is in old Delhi. Every day I come and go by bus. We are Bengalis. My mother and father live in Calcutta. I like Calcutta very much. I like Delhi too. Are you from the South? Does your wife speak Hindi? My wife speaks a little Hindi. My children speak good Hindi. Do you understand Bangla (Bengali)?

New words

rahtā hūñ	live
bhāī	brother

daftar	office
shahar	city
mujhakō pasand hai	like it
bhī	also, too
dakshiṇ	south
mausam	weather
patnī	wife
Banglā	language of Bengal
samajhate haiñ	do they understand?
har	every
roz	day
ātā-jātā	comes and goes
apane	my
parivār	family
ke sath	with
Itwār	Sunday
dekhā hai?	have you seen?

Reading exercise IV

राम — नमस्ते ।

namastē

डिक—नमस्ते।

namastē.

राम—आपका शुभ नाम?

āpkā shubh nām?

डिक—मेरा नाम डिक ब्राउन है।

mērā nām Dick Brown hai.

राम—आप भारत में कब से हैं?

āp Bhārat mēñ kab sē haiñ?

डिक—चार महीनै से।

chār mahīnē sē.

राम—आप कहां रहते हैं?

āp kahāñ rahtē haiñ?

डिक—अभी तो मैं होटल में रहता हूं।

abhī tō maiñ hōtal mēñ rahtā hūñ.

राम—किस होटल में?

kis hōtal mēñ?

डिक—जनपथ होटल में।

janpath hōtal mēñ.

राम—अच्छा होटल है?

achchhā hōtal hai?

डिक—काफ़ी अच्छा है।

kāfī achchhā hai.

राम — आप विवाहित हैं?

āp vivāhit haiñ?

डिक — जी हां । मेरे दो बच्चे भी हैं ।

jī hāñ. mērē dō bachchē bhī haiñ.

राम — वे कहां हैं?

vē kahāñ haiñ?

डिक — अभी तो वे अमरीका में हैं ।

abhī tō vē Amarīkā meñ haiṇ.

राम — वे भारत नहीं आएंगे?

vē Bhārat nahīñ āyēnge?

डिक — ज़रूर आएंगे, जब मुझको घर मिलेगा ।

zarūr āyēngē jab mujhkō ghar milēgā.

राम — आपको घर कहाँ चाहिए?

āpkō ghar kahāñ chāhiē?

डिक — सुन्दर नगर, जोरबाग, कहीं भी ।

Sundar Nagar, Jorbag, kahīñ bhī.

राम — कैसा घर चाहिए?

kaisā ghar chāhⁱye?

डिक — कम-से-कम पाँच कमरे होने चाहिए ।
नौकरों के लिए भी कमरे होने चाहिए ।

kam-se-kam pānch kamarē hōnē chāhiē.
naukarōñ kē liyē bhī kamarē hōnē chāhiē.

राम — शायद मैं आपकी मदद कर सकूं ।
shāyad maiñ āpkī madad kar sakūn.

डिक — बड़ी मेहरबानी होगी । लेकिन मैं आपको तकलीफ़ नहीं देना चाहता ।
baṛī meharbānī hōgī. lēkin maiñ āpkō taklīf nahīñ dēnā chāhatā.

राम — तकलीफ़ की कोई बात नहीं ।
taklīf kī kōī bāt nahīñ.

डिक — अच्छी बात है । आपको कोई अच्छा घर मालूम है?
achchhī bāt hai, āpkō kōī achchhā ghar mālūm hai?

राम — मैं आपको अपने साथ ले चलूंगा ।
दो-चार घर दिखाऊंगा
maiñ āpkō apnē sāth lē chalūngā.
do-char ghar dikhāūngā.

English translation

Ram — Namaste.
Dick — Namaste.
Ram — What is your name, please?
Dick — My name is Dick Brown.

Ram – How long have you been in India?
Dick – For four months.
Ram – Where do you live?
Dick – At the moment I am staying in a hotel.
Ram – In which hotel?
Dick – In Janpath hotel.
Ram – Is it a good hotel?
Dick – It is quite good.
Ram – Are you married?
Dick – Yes. I have two children.
Ram – Where are they?
Dick – At the moment they are in America.
Ram – Won't they come to India.
Dick – They certainly will, when I get a house.
Ram – Where do you want the house?
Dick – Sundar Nagar, Jorbag, anywhere.
Ram – What sort of a house do you want?
Dick – There should be at least five rooms. There should be rooms for servants too.

Ram – May be I can help you.

Dick – That will be very kind. But I don't want to trouble you.

Ram – There is no trouble at all.

Dick – Okay then. Do you know of any good house?

Ram – I shall take you with me. (I shall) show you a few houses.

New Words

kab sē	since when
vivāhit	married
abhī tō	at the moment
kaisā	what sort of
kam-se-kam	minimum, at least
shāyad	perhaps
taklīf (F)	trouble
mālūm	known
do-chār	idiomatic way of saying a few

Reading Exercise V

बरसात *barsāt*

गरमी के बाद बरसात आती है।

garmī kē bād barsāt ātī hai.

बरसात जुलाई से सितम्बर तक रहती है।

barsāt July sē Sitambar tak rahtī hai.

बरसात का मौसम स्वास्थ्य के लिए अच्छा नहीं है।

barsāt kā mausam svāsthya kē liyē achchhā nahīñ hai.

बीमारियाँ फैलती हैं।

bīmāriyāñ phailatī haiñ.

मक्खी-मच्छर बहुत परेशान करते हैं।

makkhī-machchhar bahut parēshān kartē haiñ.

कीड़े-मकोड़े भी बहुत ज्यादा हो जाते हैं।

kiṛē-makoṛē bhī bahut zyādā hō jātē haiñ.

सब्जी-तरकारी भी अच्छी नहीं मिलती।

sabzī-tarkārī bhī achchhī nahīñ milatī.

सड़कों पर पानी भर जाता है।

saṛkōñ par pānī bhar jātā hai.

लेकिन बरसात बहुत ज़रूरी भी तो है।

lēkin barsāt bahut zarūrī bhī tō hai.

बारिश की पहली बौछार कितनी अच्छी लगती है।

bārish kī pahlī bauchhār kitnī achchhī lagatī hai.

लोग चैन की साँस लेते हैं।

lōg chain kī sāns lētē haiñ.

बच्चे पेड़ो से अमरूद और जामुन तोड़ कर खाते हैं।

bachchē pēṛōñ sē amrūd aur jamun tōṛ kār khātē haiñ.

बरसात में खाने-पीने में बहुत सावधान रहना चाहिए।

barsāt mēñ khānē-pīnē mēñ bahut sāvadhān rahnā chāhiē.

बाजार की चीज़ें नहीं खानी चाहिए।

bāzār kī chīzēñ nahīñ khānī chāhiē.

उबला पानी पीना चाहिए।

ubalā pānī pīnā chāhiē.

English translation

The Rainy Season

The rainy season comes after summer.
The rainy season lasts from July to September.

The rainy season is not good for health.
Diseases spread.
Flies and mosquitoes annoy a lot.
There are too many insects too.
Good vegetables are not available.
Roads are full of water.
But the rain is also very essential.
How pleasant are the first showers of rains.
People heave a sigh of relief.
Children pluck guavas and rose apples from trees and eat.
One should be very careful about what one eats and drinks in the rainy season.
One should not eat bazaar things.
Boiled water should be taken.

New words

kē bād	after
sē	from
tak	up to
svāsthya	health
phailatī hai	spread
makkhī	flies
machchhar	mosquitoes

(they are often used as a compound word मक्खी-मच्छर *makkhi-machchhar* to mean both)

kīṛē	insects
makōṛē	spiders

(Note the compound word *kīṛē-makōṛē*)

sabzī	green vegetables
tarkārī	general term for vegetables

(Note the compound words)

bhar jātā hai	gets filled
zarūrī	essential
pahlī	first
bauchhār	showers
kitanī	how much
chain	relief
sāns	breath
amarūd	guavas
jāmun	rose apple
toṛ kar	pluck
khānā-pīnā	eating-drinking
ubalā (int. v)	boiled

Reading excrcise VI

गोपाल—आप राम को जानते हैं?

āp Rām kō jānatē haiñ?

हरी—जी नहीं, मैं नहीं जानता।

jī nahīñ, maiñ nahīñ janatā.

गोपाल—वह आपके पड़ौस में रहता है।

vah āpkē parōs mēñ rahtā hai.

हरी—मुझको अफसोस है कि मैं उससे कभी नहीं मिला।

mujhakō afsōs hai ki maiñ usasē kabhī nahīñ milā.

गोपाल—आप उससे जरूर मिलिए। वह मेरा दोस्त है।

āp usasē zarūr miliyē. vah mērā dost hai.

हरी—ज़रूर मिलूँगा।

zarūr milungā.

गोपाल—राम बहुत दिलचस्प आदमी है।

Ram bahut dilchasp ādamī hai.

हरी—बहुत अच्छी बात है।

bahut achchhī bāt hai.

गोपाल—मैं राम को पिछले पंद्रह सालों से जानता हूं।

maiñ Ram kō pichhalē pandṛah sālōñ sē jānatā hūñ.

हरी—क्या आप साथ-साथ पढ़ते थे?

kyā āp sāth-sāth paṛhate thē?

गोपाल—जी हां, हम एक ही कालिज में पढ़ते थे।

jī hāñ, ham ēk hī kaulij mēñ paṛhte thē.

हरी—कृपा कर के उनका पता दीजिए। उनके मकान का नंबर क्या है?

kripā kar kē unakā patā dījiyē. unakē makān kā nambar kyā hai?

गोपाल—नंबर तो मुझको याद नहीं है।

nambar tō mujhakō yād nahīñ hai.

हरी—अच्छा, कल बता दीजिए।

achchhā, kāl batā dījiē.

गोपाल—उसका बड़ा-सा सफेद मकान है। उसके दरवाजे पर पीपल का पेड़ है।

usakā baṛā-sā safēd makān hai. usakē darvāzē par pīpal kā peṛ hai.

हरी — मैं ढूंढने की कोशिश करूंगा।

maiñ dhūndhanē kī kōshish karūngā.

गोपाल — उसके घर का फाटक हरा है।

usakē ghar kā phāṭak harā hai.

हरी — अच्छा याद रखूंगा। आप भी मेरे साथ चलिए।

achchhā yād rakhungā. āp bhī mērē sāth chaliē.

गोपाल — हां, यह ठीक है। चलिए, मैं आपके साथ चलता हूँ।

hāñ, yah ṭhīk hai. chalie, maiñ āpkē sāth chalatā hūñ.

Gopal—Do you know Ram?

Hari—No, I don't know.

Gopal—He lives in your neighbourhood.

Hari—I am sorry that I have never met him.

Gopal—Do meet him definitely. He is my friend.

Hari—I shall definitely meet him.

Gopal—Ram is a very interesting man.

Hari—That's very good.

Gopal—I have known Ram for the last fifteen years.

Hari—Did you study together?

Gopal—Yes, we studied in the same college.

Hari—Please give me his address. What is his house number?

Gopal—I don't remember the number.

Hari—Okay. Tell me tomorrow.

Gopal—His is a big and white house. There is a pipul tree at the gate.

Hari—I shall try to locate it.

Gopal—The gate of his house is green.

Hari—Okay. I shall remember it. You come with me too.

Gopal—That is right. Come, I shall come with you.

New Words

paṛōs	neighbourhood
jānatē haiñ	do you know
mujhakō afsōs hai	I am sorry

kabhī nahīñ	never
milā	met
dōst	friend
dilchasp	interesting
pichhalē	last, (bygone)
salōñ	years
sāth-sāth	together
ēk hi	the same
kripā kar kē	please, kindly
patā	address
dījiē	give
yād nahīñ hai	don't remember
batā	tell
pīpal	a kind of tree
dhūndhnā	search for
kōshish karūngā	shall try
phāṭak	gate
yād rakhūngā	shall remember
mērē sāth	with me

Reading exercise VII

हरी—आप कहाँ गए थे?

āp kahāñ gayē thē?

गोपाल—मैं बाज़ार गया था ।

maiñ bāzār gayā thā.

हरी—आप कैसे गये थे? गाड़ी में?

āp kaisē gayē thē? Gāṛī meñ?

गोपाल—जी नहीं, मैं बस में गया था ।

jī nahīñ, maiñ bas meñ gayā thā.

हरी—आपकी गाड़ी कहाँ है?

āpkī gāṛī kahāñ hai?

गोपाल—गाड़ी खराब है, इसलिए मैं बस में गया ।

gāṛī kharāb hai isliyē maiñ bas meñ gayā.

हरी—आज दूकानें खुली हैं?

āj dūkānēñ khulī haiñ?

गोपाल—जी हां, सब दूकानें खुली हैं ।

jī hāñ, sab dūkāñē khulīñ haiñ.

हरी—मुझको परदे का कपड़ा खरीदना है ।

mujhakō pardē kā kapṛā kharīdanā hai.

गोपाल—बाजार मेरे घर के पीछे ही है ।

bāzār mērē ghar kē pīchhē hī hai.

हरी—तो फिर आप बस में क्यों गए थे?

tō phir āp bas mēñ kyoñ gayē thē?

गोपाल—मैं तो सब्जी-मंडी गया था।

maiñ tō sabzī manḍī gayā thā.

हरी—मेरे घर के सामने बाग है।

mērē ghar kē sāmanē bāg hai.

गोपाल—शाम को बाग में बच्चे खेलते हैं।

shām kō bāg meñ bachchē khelatē haiñ.

हरी—मेरे बच्चे घर के अन्दर ही खेलते हैं।

mērē bachchē ghar kē andar hī khelatē haiñ.

गोपाल—उनको बाग में खेलना पसन्द नहीं है?

unkō bāg mēñ khelanā pasand nahiñ hai?

हरी—जी नहीं। अपने बच्चों को मेरे घर भेजिए।

jī nahiñ. apnē bachchōñ kō mērē ghar bhējiyē.

गोपाल—मैं आया तो बाहर का दरवाज़ा खुला था।

maiñ āyā tō bāhar kā darvāzā khulā thā.

हरी — किसने खोला?

kisanē khōlā?

गोपाल — मैं नहीं जानता। शायद नौकर ने खुला छोड़ दिया था।

maiñ nahīñ jānatā. shāyad naukar nē khulā chhoṛ diyā thā.

हरी — नौकर बहुत लापरवाह है।

naukar bahut lāparvāh hai.

गोपाल — आज कल बहुत चोरियां होती हैं।

ājkal bahut chōriyāñ hōtī haiñ.

हरी — लेकिन मेरा नौकर बिल्कुल नहीं समझता।

lēkin mērā naukar bilkul nahīñ samajhatā.

New Words

gāṛī	car
khulī	open
pardē kā kapṛā	curtain material
ghar kē pichhē	behind the house
sabzi mandi	wholesale vegetable market
sāmnē	in front

khelatē haiñ	play
andar	inside
bhējiyē	send
lāparvāh	careless
chōriyāñ	thefts
samajhatē	understands

Reading exercise VIII

यह गुलाब लाल है। इसकी पत्तियाँ हरी हैं। मेरे बाग में कई रंग के गुलाब हैं—पीले, गुलाबी, सफ़ेद और लाल। मेरे बाग में फल के भी बहुत पेड़ हैं। मेरा माली होशियार और मेहनती है। वह सारा दिन बाग में काम करता है। वह ईमानदार भी है। उसके कई छोटे-छोटे बच्चे हैं। वह काफी गरीब है। उसकी पत्नी भी मेरे घर में काम करती है। वह कुछ-कुछ सुस्त है। माली के बच्चे बहुत दुबले-पतले हैं। अकसर बीमार रहते हैं।

आजकल मौसम अच्छा नहीं है। बाज़ार में तरकारियाँ बहुत मंहगी है। फल भी मंहगे है। कोई चीज़ सस्ता नहीं है। माली के बच्चे समझदार है। बाज़ार की गंदी चीज़ें नहीं खाते।

yah gulāb lāl hai. isakī pattiyāñ harī haiñ. mērē bāg meñ kaī rang kē gulāb haiñ—pīlē, gulābī, safēd aur lāl. mērē bāg meñ phal kē bhī bahut pēṛ haiñ. mērā mālī hōshiyar aur mehantī hai. vah sārā din bāg mēñ kām karatā hai. vah imāndār bhī hai. usakē kaī chhotē-chhotē bachchē haiñ. vah kāfī arīb hai. usakī patnī bhī mērē ghar mēñ kām karatī hai. vah kuchchh-kuchchh sust hai. mālī ke bachchē bahut dubalē-patalē haiñ. aksar bīmār rahtē haiñ.

ājkal mausam achchhā nahīñ hai. bāzār mēñ tarkāriyāñ bahut mahangī haiñ. phal bhī mahangē haiñ. koī chīz sastī nahīñ hai. mālī kē bachchē samajhdār haiñ. bāzār kī gandī chīzēñ nahīñ khāte.

New Words

gulāb	rose
lāl	red
pattiyāñ	leaves
pīlē	yellow
gulābī	pink
safēd	white
bahut	many
pēṛ	tree
mālī	gardener
hōshiyār	intelligent, competent

mehnatī	hard working
kaī	several
chhōṭē chhōṭē	small-small
kāfī	quite
garīb	poor
kām karatī hai	works
dubalē-patalē	lean and thin
tarkāriyāñ	vegetables
mahangī	expensive
chīz	thing
sastē	cheap
samajhadār	sensible
gandī	dirty, unclean
nahīñ khātē	don't eat

CHAPTER NINE

A MINIMAL DICTIONARY

Greetings

namaste	*namastē*
namaskar	*namaskār*

Time

day	*din* (M)
morning	*savērā* (M)
afternoon	*dōpahar* (F)
evening	*shām* (F)
night	*rāt* (F)
week	*haftā, saptāh* (M)
fortnight	*pakhwāṛā* (M)
month	*mahīnā, mās* (M)
year	*sāl, varsh* (M)
decade	*dashak* (M)
century	*sadī, shatābdī* (F)
today	*āj* (M)
yesterday	*kal* (M)
tomorrow	*kal* (M)
the day before yesterday	*parsōn̐* (M)
the day after tomorrow	*parsōn̐* (M)

Numbers

one	*ēk*
two	*dō*
three	*tīn*
four	*chār*
five	*pañch*
six	*chhe*
seven	*sāt*
eight	*āṭh*
nine	*nau*
ten	*das*
eleven	*gyārah*
twelve	*bārah*
thirteen	*tērah*
fourteen	*chaudah*
fifteen	*pandrah*
sixteen	*sōlah*
seventeen	*satrah*
eighteen	*athārah*
nineteen	*unnīs*
twenty	*bīs*

Ordinal numbers

first	*pahlā*
second	*dūsarā*
third	*tīsarā*
fourth	*chauthā.*
fifth	*panchvāñ*
sixth	*chhaṭhā*
seventh	*satavāñ*
eighth	*āṭhvāñ*

ninth	*nauvāñ*
tenth	*dasavāñ*
eleventh	*gyārahvāñ*
twelfth	*bārahvāñ*
thirteenth	*tērahvāñ*
fourteenth	*chaudahvāñ*
fifteenth	*pandrahvāñ*
sixteenth	*sōlahvāñ*
seventeeth	*satrahvāñ*
eighteenth	*athārahvāñ*
nineteenth	*unnīsvāñ*
twentieth	*bisvāñ*
hundredth	*sauvāñ*
thousandth	*hazārvāñ*
dozen	*darjan*
half a dozen	*ādhā darjan*

Planet

sun	*sūrya*
moon	*chandra*
mars	*mangal*
neptune	*budh*
jupiter	*bṛhaspati*
venus	*shukra*
saturn	*shani*

Days of the week

days of the week	*vār* (M)
sunday	*itvār* or *ravivar*
monday	*sōmvār*
tuesday	*mangalvār*
wednesday	*budhvār*

thursday	*brihaspativār* (for short also called *birvār*)
friday	*shukravār*
saturday	*shanivār* (also called *shanichar*)

Directions

direction	*aishā* (F)
east	*pūrva* (M)
west	*pashchim* (M)
north	*uttar* (M)
south	*dakshiṇ* (M)

Human body

ankle	*ṭakhanā* (M)
arm	*bānh* (F)
armpit	*bagal* (F)
back	*piṭh* (F)
beard	*dāṛhī* (F)
blood	*khūn* (M)
body	*sharīr* (M)
bone	*haḍḍī* (F)
brain	*dimāg* (M)
breast (woman's)	*stan* (M)
cheek	*gāl* (M)
chest	*chhātī* (F)
chin	*ṭhoḍi* (F)
ear	*kān* (M)
elbow	*kōhnī* (F)
eye	*ānkh* (F)
eyeball	*putali* (F)

eyebrow	*bhãũñ* (F)
eyelashes	*palak* (F)
face	*chēhrā* (M)
finger	*anguli* (F)
finger-nail	*nākhūn* (M)
flesh	*māns* (M)
foot	*pair* (M)
forehead	*māṭhā* (M)
hand	*hāth* (M)
head	*sir* (M)
heart	*dil, hridaya* (M)
hair	*bāl* (M)
heel	*ēdi* (F)
kidney	*gurdā* (M)
lip	*hōṭh* (M)
liver	*jigar* (M)
lung	*phēpharā* (M)
moustache	*mūchh* (F)
mouth	*mūh* (M)
neck	*garden* (F)
nail	*nākhūn* (M)
nose	*nāk* (F)
palm	*hathēli* (F)
shoulder	*kandhā*
skin	*chamri*
skull	*khopaṛi* (F)
spine	*riṛh* (F)
stomach	*pēṭ* (M)
teeth	*dānt* (M)
thigh	*iāngh* (F)
toe	*pair-ki-anguli* (F)
tongue	*jibh* (F)

throat	*galā* (M)
thumb	*angūṭhā* (M)
vein	*nas* (F)
waist	*kamar* (F)
wrist	*kalāi* (F)

Animals

animal	*jānvar* (M)
bear	*bhālū* (M)
buffalo	*bhains* (F), *bhainsa* (M)
bullock	*bail* (M)
cat	*billi* (F)
camel	*ūnt* (M) *ūntni* (F)
cow	*gāe* (F)
calf	*bachhṛā* (M) *bachhiā* (F)
deer	*hiran* (M)
dog	*kuttā* (M)
bitch	*kutiā* (F)
donkey	*gadhā* (M)
elephant	*hāthi* (F), *hathini* (M)
fox	*lomṛi* (F)
goat	*bakari* (M) *backarā* (F)
horse	*ghorā* (M)
mare	*ghori* (F)
mule	*tattū*
monkey	*bandar* (M)
mouse	*chūhā* (M)
lamb	*memnā* (M & F)
lion	*simha, babar shēr* (M)
lioness	*simhani*
python	*ajgar* (M)
snake	*sanp*

sheep	*bhēṛ* (F)
skunk	*chhachhundar* (M)
squirrel	*gilahrī* (F)
tiger	*shēr* (M)
tigress	*shērnī* (F)

Birds

Bat	*chamgādaṛ* (M)
Bird	*pakshī, chiṛiyā* (M)
Crow	*kauā* (M)
Cock	*murgā* (M)
Crane	*sāras* (M)
Cuckoo	*kōyal* (F)
Duck	*batakh* (F)
Hen	*murgī* (F)
Kite	*chīl* (F)
Nightingale	*bulbul* (F)
owl	*ullū* (M)
partridge	*tītar* (M)
parrot	*tōtā* (M)
peacock	*mōr* (M)
pigeon	*kabūtar* (M)
sparrow	*gauraiyā* (F)
swan	*hans* (M)
vulture	*giddha* (M)

Fish and water animals

crab	*kēkṛā* (M)
crocodile	*magar* (M)
fish	*machhlī* (M)
leech	*jōnk* (F)
tortoise	*kachhuā* (M)

Insects

ant	*chinṭi* (F)
ant (white)	*dīmak* (F)
bee	*mdhumakkhi* (F)
bug	*khatmal* (M)
butterfly	*titlī* (F)
fly	*makkhī* (F)
frog	*mēndhak* (M)
germs	*kitaṇu* (M)
glow worm	*juganu* (M)
insect	*kiṛā* (M)
lizard	*chhipkalī* (F)
locust	*ṭiḍḍī* (F)
mosquito	*machchhar* (M)
scorpion	*bichchhū* (M)
spider	*makṛī* (F)

Food stuff

bread	*rōṭī* (F), *chapātī* (F)
butter	*makkhan* (M)
butter-milk	*chhāchh* (M)
cashewnut	*kājū* (M)
chicken	*murgī* (F)
clarified butter	*ghē* (M)
coconut (green)	*nāriyal* (M)
coconut (dry)	*khōprā* (M)
coffee	*kaufī* (F)
cottage cheese	*panīr* (M)
corn	*makkā* (M)
curd	*dahī* (M)
dates	*khajūr* (M)
dry fruit	*mēvā* (F)

egg	*aṇḍā* (M)
fish	*machhalī* (F)
flour (whole wheat)	*āṭā* (M)
flour (white)	*maidā* (F)
gram	*chanā* (M)
jaggery	*gūṛ* (M)
lentils	*dāl* (F)
milk	*dūdh* (M)
oil	*tēl* (M)
pickle	*achār* (M)
rice	*chāval* (M)
salt	*namak* (M)
sugar	*chīnī* (F)
wheat	*gēhūñ* (M)

Vegetables

beans (green)	*sēm* (F)
beans (string)	*lōbiyā* (F)
beans (French)	*farās bean* (F)
cabbage	*ƀandgōbhī* (F)
carrot	*gājar* (F)
cauliflower	*phūlgōbhī* (F)
coriander (green)	*harā dhaniā* (M)
cucumber	*khīrā* (M)
eggplant	*ƀaingan* (M)
garlic	*lahsun* (M)
lime, lemon	*niƀ* [illegible] (M)
mint	*pu*[illegible]*inā* (F)
onion	*py*[illegible]*z* (M)
okra	*ƀhin*[illegible]*ī* (F)
peas	*maṭa*[illegible] (F)
pepper (green)	*shimlā mirch* (F)

potato	*ālū* (M)
pumpkin (red)	*kaddū* (M)
radish	*mūli* (M)
spinach	*pālak* (M)
sweet potato	*shakarkand* (F)
tomato	*ṭamāṭar* (M)
turnip	*shalgam* (F)

Fruits

apple	*sēb* (M)
apricot	*khūmāni* (F)
banana	*kēlā* (F)
custard apple	*sharīfā* (M)
grapes	*angūr* (M)
guava	*amrūd* (M)
mango	*ām* (M)
melon	*kharbūzā* (M)
orange	*santarā* (M)
papaya	*papītā* (M)
peach	*āḍū* (M)
pear	*nāshpāti* (M)
pineapple	*anannās* (M)
pomegranate	*anār* (M)
watermelon	*tarbūz* (*M*)

Spices and condiments

aniseed	*saunf* (M)
asafoatida	*hing* (F)
bayleaf	*tejpatta* (M)
cardamom (white)	*chhōṭi elaichi* (F)
cardamom (black)	*baḍi elaichi* (F)
chillies (red)	*lāl mirch* (F)

cinnamon	*dālchīnī* (F)
cloves	*laung* (M)
coriander	*dhania* (M)
cumin	*zeera* (M)
fenugreek	*mēthī* (F)
garlic	*lahsun* (M)
ginger	*adrakh* (F)
mace	*jāvitrī* (F)
mint	*pudīnā* (M)
mustard	*rā-ī* (F)
nutmeg	*jāyaphal* (M)
pepper (green)	*harī mirch* (F)
pepper (black)	*kālī mirch* (F)
saffron	*kēsar* (F)
salt	*namak* (M)
sesame	*til* (M)
spice	*masālā* (M)
tamarind	*imlī* (F)
turmeric	*haldī* (F)

Weights and measures

kilogram	*kilō* (M)
gram	*gram* (M)
scale	*tarāzū* (F)
weight	*vazan* (M)
heavy	*bhārī* (ad)
light	*halkā* (ad)
litre	*litre* (M)
measurement	*nāp* (M)
metre	*miṭar* (M)
half	*ādhā*
one quarter	*ēk-chauthā-ī*

one third	*ēk-tihā-ī*
three quarters	*teen-chauthāī*
to add	*joṛnā*
to substract	*ghaṭānā*
to multiply	*guṇā karnā*
to divide	*bhāg karnā*

Minerals, metals and precious stones

mineral	*khanij* (M)
metal	*dhātu* (F)
precious stone	*ratna* (M)
brass	*pītal* (M)
bronze	*kānsā* (M)
copper	*tāmbā* (M)
gold	*sōnā* (M)
silver	*chāndī* (F)
steel	*ispāt* (M)
alum	*phiṭakari* (F)
chalk	*khaṛiyā* (F)
clay	*miṭṭī* (F)
glass	*shīshā* (M)
iron	*lōhā* (M)
lime	*chūnā* (M)
marble	*sangmarmar* (M)
mercury	*pārā* (M)
coral	*mūngā* (M)
diamond	*hīrā* (M)
emerald	*pannā* (M)
pearl	*mōṭī* (M)
ruby	*lāl mānik* (M)
sapphire (blue)	*nīlam* (M)
topaz	*pukharāj* (M)

Around the house

basket	*tokaṛī* (F)
bathroom	*gusalkhānā* (M)
bed	*palang* (M)
bedcover	*palangpōsh* (M)
bedsheet	*chādar* (F)
bottle	*botal* (F)
bucket	*balaṭī* (F)
candle	*mōmbattī* (F)
carpet	*kālīn, galīchā*
ceiling	*chhat* (F)
chair	*kursī* (F)
comb	*kanghā,, kanghī* (M & F)
cupboard	*almārī* (F)
curtain	*pardā* (M)
dining room	*khānē-kā-kamarā* (M)
dining table	*khānē-kī-mēz* (F)
divan	*divān* (M)
drawing room	*baiṭhak* (M)
floor	*farsh* (F)
floor rug	*kālīn* (F)
guest room	*mehmān-kā-kamarā* (M)
kitchen	*rasōī*
key	*chābī* (F)
lock	*tālā* (M)
mattress	*gaddā* (M)
mat	*chatā-ī* (F)
mirror	*shīshā*
needle	*suī* (F)
pillow	*takiyā* (M)
scissors	*kainchī* (F)

sieve	*chhalanī* (F)
strainer	*chhannī* (F)
study	*paṛhnē-kā-kamarā* (M)
soap	*sābun*
table (dining)	*khānē kī-mēz* (F)
table (writing)	*likhanē-kī-mēz* (F)
thread	*dhāgā* (M)
umbrella	*chhātā, chhatarī* (F)
utensils	*bartan* (M)
varandah	*barāmadā* (M)
wall	*dīvār* (F)
window	*khiṛkī* (F)

Around the town

airport	*havāi aḍḍā* (M)
building	*imārat* (F)
bullock cart	*bailgaṛī* (F)
church	*girjāghar* (M)
college	*college* (M)
crowd	*bhīr* (F)
ditch	*khad, khāī* (F)
electricity	*bijlī* (F)
farm	*khēt, fārm* (M)
fence	*bāṛā* (M)
field	*maidān, khēt*
garden	*bāg, bagīchā*
gutter	*nālā* (M)
hawker	*phērīwālā*
highway	*baṛī saṛak* (F)
hospital	*aspatāl* (M)
hotel	*hotal* (M)
hut	*jhōnprī* (F)

inn	*sarāe* (F)
intersection (roads)	*c aurāhā* (M)
land	*amin* (F)
lane	*gali* (F)
library	*pustakālaya*
main market	*baṛā bazār* (M)
market	*bazār* (M)
pole (electric)	*bijli-kā-khambhā*
post	*ḍak* (F)
postman	*ḍākiyā* (M)
post office	*ḍākghar* (M)
railway station	*railway station*
restaurant	*restōrān* (M)
road	*saṛak* (F)
school	*skūl* (M)
sewage	*nālā*
shop	*dūkān* (M)
shopkeeper	*dūkāndār* (M)
taxi	*taiksi* (F)
telephone	*telifon* (M)
telegraph office	*tārghar* (M)
telegram	*tār* (M)
university	*vishvavidyālaya* (M)
zoo	*chiṛiyāghar* (M)

Trades and professions

artisan	*kārigar* (M & F)
astrologer	*jyotishi* (M & F)
author	*lekhak, lekhikā* (M & F)
barber	*nā-i* (M)
blacksmith	*luhār* (M)
butcher	*kasā-i* (M)

carpenter	*baṛhai* (M)
cook	*rasōiyā, khānsāmā* (M)
dyer	*rangrēz* (M)
farmer	*kisān* (M)
gardener	*māli* (M)
goldsmith	*sunār* (M)
jeweller	*jauhari* (M)
labourer	*mazdūr* (M)
merchant	*vyāpāri* (M)
milkman	*gvālā* *dūdhvālā* (M)
nurse	*nurse* (F)
potter	*kumhār*
servant	*naukar* (M)
servant (maid)	*naukarānī* (F)
sweeper	*jamādār* (M)
sweet vendor	*halwāī*
printer	*mudrak* (M)
publisher	*prakāshak*
tailor	*darzī* (M)
teacher	*shikshak* (M), *adhyapak* (M) *guru* (M)
teacher (lady)	*shikshikā, adhyāpikā, guru* (also teacher)
washerman	*dhōbī* (M)
weaver	*julāhā*, (M) *bunkar*

The Seasons

rainy season	*barsāt* (F)
spring	*basant* (F)
summer	*garmī* (F)

winter	*jāṛā* (M)
rain	*bārish* (F)
dust-storm	*āndhī* (F)
storm	*tūfān* (M)
wind	*havā* (F)
sun (heat)	*dhūp* (F)
chill	*ṭhanḍ* (F)
heat	*garmī* (F)

Nature (*prakriti*)

air	*havā* (F)
atmosphere	*vātāvaran* (M)
breeze	*havā* (F)
cliff	*chattān* (F)
cloud	*bādal* (M)
current (river)	*dhārā* (F)
dawn	*us..ākāl* (M)
dark night	*andhēri rāt* (M)
new moon	*amāvas* (M)
dust	*dhūl* (F)
dust storm	*āndhī* (F)
earth	*prithvī* (F)
eclipse	*grahaṇ* (M)
fog	*kohrā* (M)
hill	*pahaṛī* (F)
hail	*ōlā* (M)
lake	*jhīl* (F)
light (sun)	*sūraj-kī-roshanī* (F)
moon	*chānd, chandra* (M)
moon (full)	*pūrṇa chandra* (M)
moon light	*chāndnī* (F)

moonlit night	*chāndni rāt* (F)
full-moon night	*pūrnimā* (F)
mountain	*pahāṛ* (M)
ocean	*mahāsāgar* (M)
peninsula	*prayadvīp* (M)
rain	*bārish, varshā* (F)
rainbow	*indradhanush* (M)
rainwater	*bārish-kā-pānī* (M)
rainy season	*barsāt* (F)
rainy day	*bārish-kā-din* (M)
rock	*chaṭṭān* (F)
sand	*bālū* (F)
sea	*samudra* (M)
seaside	*samudra-kā-kinārā* (M)
sky	*āsmān, ākāsh* (M)
snow	*barf* (E)
star	*tārā* (M)
storm	*tūfān* (F)
wave	*lahar* (F)
wind	*havā* (F)

Politics, government, etc.

administration	*prashāsan* (M)
administrator	*prashāsak* (M & F)
ambassador	*rajdūt* (M & F)
democracy	*loktantra* (M)
diplomat	*rajnayik* (M & F)
election	*chunāō* (M)
embassy	*rājdūtāvās* (M)
federation	*sangh* (M)
federal	*sanghīya* (M)
franchise	*matādhikār* (M)

government	*sarkār* (F)
governmental	*sarkārī* (F)
independence	*svadhīntā* (F)
imprisonment	*qaid* (F)
jail	*jail* (M)
judge	*nyāyādhīsh*
judgment	*faislā* (M)
justice	*nyāya* (M)
law	*kānūn* (M)
law court	*adālat* (F)
lawyer	*vakīl* (M & F)
law suit	*mukaddamā*
legal	*kānūnī* (ad)
municipality	*nagarpālikā* (F)
parliament	*saṁsad* (M)
parliament house	*saṁsad bhavan*
parliament, member of	*saṁsad sadasya*
politics	*rājnīti* (F)
political	*rājnītik*
politician	*rājnītigya* (M & F)
vote	*mat* (M)
independence day	*svādhīnatā divas*
republic day	*gaṇatantra divas*
national flag	*rāshtrīya jhaṇḍā* (M)

High offices in the country

president	*rāshṭrapati*
vice-president	*upa-rāshṭrapati*
minister	*mantrī*
minister of state	*rājya-mantrī*
deputy minister	*upa-mantrī*
secretary (to govt.)	*sachiva*

governor	*rājyapāl*
president's house	*rashṭrapati bhavan*
supreme court	*sarvōchcha nyāyālaya*
chief justice	*mukhya nyāyādhish*
cabinet	*mantrimandal*
army	*sēnā* (F)
soldier	*sainik, sipāhi* (M)
to fight	*larā-i karnā*
war	*yuddha* (M)
peace	*shānti* (F)
weapon	*hathiyār* (M)
gun	*bandūk* (F)
bomb	*bam* (M)
truce	*sandhi* (F)

Fine arts, literature, etc.

actor	*abhinētā* (M)
actress	*abhinētri* (F)
art	*kalā* (F)
artist	*kalākār* (M & F)
audience	*darshak* (M)
dance	*nāch, nritya* (M)
dancer	*nartak* (M), *nartaki* (F)
drama	*nāṭak* (M)
dramatist	*nāṭak.kār* (M & F)
essay	*nibandh* (M)
essayist	*nibandhkār* (M & F)
folk art	*lōk-kalā* (F)
instrument (musical)	*vādya* (M)
music	*sangit* (M)
musician	*sangitkār* (M & F)
novel	*upanyās* (M)

novelist	*upanyāskār* (M & F)
poet	*kavi* (M & F)
poetry	*kavitā* (F)
singer	*gāyak* (M), *gāyikā* (F)
song	*gānā, gīt* (M)
song (folk)	*lokgīt* (F)
story (folk)	*lok-kathā* (F)
story	*kahānī* (F)
storywriter	*kahānīkār* (M & F)

Sports and games

game	*khēl* (M)
sports	*khēl* (M)
sportsman	*khilārī* (M & F)
team	*teem* (F)
group	*dal* (M)
playground	*khēl-kā-maidān* (M)
to win	*jītnā*
to lose	*hārnā*

Health, illness

abdomenal pain	*pēṭ-kā-dard*
chickenpox	*mōti hara chhōtī mātā*
cold	*zukām*
cough	*khānsī*
fever	*bukhār*
malaria	*malēria*
typhoid	*miyādī bukhār*
smallpox	*chēchak*
measles	*khasrā*
pain	*dard*
swelling	*sūjan*

medicine	*davā*
medical treatment	*ilāj*
nausea	*jī machlānā*
headache	*sir-kā-dard*
whooping cough	*kālī khānsī* (F)
dysentry	*pēchish* (F)

Relationship

relationship	*rishtā*
relative	*rishtēdār*
father	*pitā, bāp*
mother	*mā, mātā*
brother	*bhāī*
sister	*bahin*
husband	*pati*
wife	*patnī*
son	*bēta, putra*
daughter	*beṭī, putrī*
nephew (brother's son)	*bhatījā*
(sister's son)	*bhānjā*
niece (brother's daughter)	*bhatījī*
(sister's daughter)	*bhānjī*
uncle (father's brother)	*chāchā*
(his wife)	*chāchī*
uncle (mother's brother)	*māmā*
(his wife)	*māmī*
brother-in-law	
(sister's husband)	*bahnōī*
(wife's brother)	*sālā*
sister-in-law	
(wife's sister)	*sālī*
(brother's wife)	*bhābhī*

father's sister	*phūphī*
(her husband)	*phūphā*
grandfather (paternal)	*dādā*
grandmother (paternal)	*dādī*
grandfather (maternal)	*nānā*
grandmother (maternal)	*nānī*
grandson (son's son)	*pōtā*
granddaughter (son's daughter)	*pōtī*
grandson (daughter's son)	*nātī*
granddaughter (daughter's daughter)	*nātin*
grandchildren	*nātī-pōtē*
family	*parivār* (M)
son-in-law	*dāmād*
daughter-in-law	*bahū*
step-mother	*sautēlī māñ*
step-father	*sautēlā bāp*

Colours

black	*kālā*
blue	*nīlā*
brown	*bhūrā*
green	*harā*
pink	*gulābī*
yellow	*pīlā*
olive	*mehdī*
orange	*nārāngī*
purple	*baingnī*
white	*safēd*

Adjectives

angry	*nārāz, gussā*
annual	*sālānā, vārshik*

any	*kōī*
bad	*burā, kharāb*
beautiful	*sundar*
better	*behtar, zyādā achchhā*
big	*baṛā*
bitter	*kaṛuvā*
blind	*andhā*
boiled	*ublā huā*
bold	*sāhasī*
brief	*sankshipta*
broad	*chauṛā*
busy	*vyast, masrūf*
calm	*shānt*
capable	*yogya, lāyak*
careless	*lāparvāh*
central	*bīch kā*
certain	*nishchit*
cheap	*sastā*
cheerful	*khush, prasanna*
clean	*sāf*
clear	*sāf*
clever	*hōshiyār*
closed	*band*
cold	*ṭhandā*
comfortable	*ārāmdēh*
common	*ām*
cooked	*pakā huā*
costly	*mahangā*
courteous	*vinayī*
cowardly	*ḍarpōk*
damp	*gīlā*
dear (loved one)	*pyārā, priya*

decent	*achchhā*
deep	*gehrā*
dense	*ghana*
different	*fark, bhinna*
difficult	*kaṭhin, mushkil*
dishonest	*bēimān*
dirty	*mailā, gandā*
distant	*dūr*
dry	*sūkhā*
dull (dim in intelligence)	*buddhū*
dull (not quick)	*sust*
dull (boring)	*ubānēvālā*
dull (colourless)	*phīkā*
early	*shuru kē*
early (you are early)	*āp jaldī ā gayē*
early (give early reply)	*jaldī jawāb dijiyē*
easy	*āsān, saral*
economic	*ārthik*
economical (frugal)	*kifāyatshār*
elder	*badā* (add *sē* before to denote comparative degree e.g. *usasē baḍā*)
empty	*khālī*
enough	*kāfi*
every	*har, prati*
fair (just)	*ucl t*
fair (complexion)	*gō*
fair (weather)	*ac. hhā, sāf*
faithful	*vafā'ār*
false	*jhūṭhā*
famous	*mashhūr, prasiddha*
fat	*moṭā*

feeble	*kamzōr*
fertile	*upajāū*
fierce	*bhayankar*
happy	*sukhī, khush*
hard	*sakht, kaṭhōr*
harsh	*sakth kaṭhōr*
hasty	*jaldbāz*
healthy	*swasth, tandarust*
heavy	*bhārī*
healthy	*swasth*
high	*ūnchā*
hollow	*pōlā*
holy	*pavitra*
honest	*imāndār*
hot	*garam*
humble	*namra*
ignorant	*agyānī*
ill	*bīmār*
imaginary	*khyālī, kālpanik*
important	*zarūrī*
innocent (naive)	*nādān, bhōlā*
innocent (of guilt)	*nirdōsh, bēkasūr*
insane	*pāgal*
interesting	*dilchasp*
jealous	*irshyālu*
lame	*langṛā*
large	*baḍā*
last	*ākhirī, antim*
late (dead)	*swargīya*
late (in time)	*dēr sē*
lazy	*ālasī, sust*
lean	*dublā*

learned	*vidvān*
light (weight)	*halkā*
little (size)	*chhoṭā*
little (quantity)	*thoṛā, kuchh*
long	*lambā*
low	*nīchā*
mad	*pāgal*
many	*bahut*
mean (person behaviour)	*nīch*
moral	*naitik*
much	*bahut*
narrow	*tang, sankrā*
national	*rashtṛiya*
natural	*kudartī*
necessary	*zarūri*
next	*dūsrā, aglā*
new	*nayā*
notorious	*badnām*
obedient	*āgyākāri*
official	*sarkārī*
old (opp. of new)	*purānā*
old (age)	*buddḥā*
only	*kēval, sirf*
open	*khulā*
other	*dūsarā*
patient	*sabradār, dhairyavān*
peaceful	*shānt*
quiet	*shānt*
rapid	*tēz*
raw	*kachchā*
real	*sachchā*

religious	*dhārmik*
respectful	*sammanpūrṇa*
respected	*sammānit*
rich	*amīr, dhanī*
right (correct)	*ṭhīk*
right (hand)	*dāhinā, dāyāñ*
ripe	*pakkā*
rough (texture)	*khurdurā*
round	*gōl*
rude	*badtamīz*
rural	*dēhātī*
sacred	*pavitra*
sad	*udās, dukhī*
safe	*surakshit*
same	*vahī, vaisā hī*
secret	*gupta, rahasya*
severe	*sakht, kahṭōr*
shallow	*chhichhlā*
sharp	*tēz*
short (brief)	*chhōṭā*
short (stature)	*nāṭā*
silken	*reshamī*
slow (speed)	*dhīrē*
slow (backward, not smart)	*pīchhē, sust*
small	*chhōṭā*
social	*sāmājik*
soft	*naram, mulāyam*
solid	*ṭhōs*
some	*kuchh*
sour	*khaṭṭā*
special	*khās*

stale	*bāsi*
strange	*vichitra, ajīb*
strong	*mazbūt*
stupid	*bevakūf, mūrkh*
successful	*saphal*
such	*aisā*
sure	*nishchit*
sweet	*mīṭhā*
swift	*tēz*
tasty	*svādishṭ*
tender	*naram, mulāyam*
thick	*moṭā*
thin (person, animal)	*dublā*
thin (neuter gender)	*patlā*
thirsty	*pyāsā*
tight	*tang, kasa*
tired	*thakā*
true	*sach*
ugly	*badsūrat*
vain	*ghamanḍī*
weak	*kamzōr*
wily	*chālāk*
wise	*buddhimān*
zealous	*utsāhī*

Verbs

to accept	*manzūr karnā, svikār karnā*
to admire	*prashansā karnā*
to advise	*salāh dēnā, rāe dēnā*
to answer	*javāb dēnā*
to argue	*bahas karnā*
to arrange	*intazām karnā*

to arrive	*pahunchnā*
to arrest	*giraftār karnā*
to ask	*puchhnā*
to attack	*hamlā karnā*
to attempt	*kōshish karnā*
to awake	*jāganā*
to be	*hōnā*
to be afraid	*darnā*
to be angry	*nārāz hōnā, gussā hōnā*
to be tired	*thakā hōnā*
to bathe	*nahānā, snān karnā*
to bear (tolerate)	*sahnā*
to bear the burden	*bhar uṭhanā*
to become	*hōnā, hōjānā*
to beat	*mārnā, piṭnā*
to beat (egg)	*phēnṭnā*
to beg	*bhīkh māngnā*
to begin	*shurū karnā*
to believe	*vishvās karn*
to bite	*kaṭnā*
to blame	*dōsh dēnā*
to boil (tr.)	*ubālnā*
to boil (int.)	*ubālnā*
to break (tr.)	*tōṛnā*
to break (int.)	*tūṭnā*
to breath	*sāns lenā*
to bring	*lānā*
to build	*banānā*
to burn (tr.)	*jalna*
to burn (int.)	*jalānā*
to burst	*phaṛnā*
to burst (int.)	*phūṭna*

to buy	*kharidnā*
to call	*bulānā*
to care	*parvāh karnā*
to carry	*uṭhānā*
to catch	*pakaṛnā*
to change	*badalnā*
to change (int.)	*badal jānā*
to chop	*chhōṭē ṭukṛē kaṭnā*
to clean	*sāf karnā*
to climb	*charḥnā*
to desire	*chāhnā*
to die	*marnā*
to dig	*khōdnā*
to dine	*khānā*
to do	*karnā*
to doubt	*shak karnā, sandeh karnā*
to draw	*khīnchnā*
to dream	*sapnā dekhnā*
to dress	*kapṛē pehan-nā*
to drink	*pīnā*
to drive (a car)	*moṭar chalānā*
to dry (tr.)	*sukhānā*
to dry (int.)	*sukhanā*
to eat	*khānā*
to exclaim	*chillānā*
to explain	*samjhānā*
to excuse	*māf karnā*
to examine	*parīkshā karna, jānchnā*
to fall	*girnā*
to fear	*ḍarnā*
to feed	*khilānā*
to feel	*anubhava karnā*

to fight	*laṛnā*
to fill	*bharnā*
to find	*pānā*
to finish	*khatam karnā*
to forget	*b. lnā*
to forgive	*mā, karnā*
to freeze	*jam..nā*
to freeze (int.)	*jamnā*
to fry	*talnā*
to get	*pānā*
to get up	*uṭhnā*
to give	*dēnā*
to give up	*chhōṛ dēnā*
to go	*jānā*
to go in	*andar jānā*
to go out	*bāhār jānā*
to get out	*bāhar nikalnā*
to grind	*p nā*
to grow	*arḥnā*
to guide	*rāstā dikhānā*
to increase	*baṛhnā*
to insult	*apmān karnā*
to irrigate	*sinchnā*
to irritate	*nārāz karnā*
to introduce	*parichay karānā*
to joke	*mazāk karnā*
to jump	*kūdanā*
to keep	*rakhnā*
to kick	*lāth mārnā*
to kill	*jān sē mārnā, mār dālnā*
to kiss	*chūmna*
to know	*janaṇā*

to laugh	*hansnā*
to lay the table	*mēz lagānā*
to lead (the way)	*rāstā dikhānā, āgē-āgē chalnā*
to learn	*sīkhnā*
to lend	*udhār dēnā*
to lie down	*lēṭnā*
to lie (telling)	*jhūṭh bōlnā*
to lift	*uṭhānā*
to like	*pasand karnā*
to look	*dēkhnā*
to lose	*khōnā*
to love	*pyār karnā*
to make	*banānā*
to marry	*shādī karnā*
to measure	*nāpanā*
to meet	*milnā*
to memorize	*raṭnā*
to move	*sarkanā*
to move (int.)	*sarkānā*
to move on	*āgē sarkānā*
to obey	*kahnā mānanā*
	āgyā mānanā
to object	*āpatti karnā*
to offend	*nārāz karnā*
to open	*khōlnā*
to open (int.)	*khulnā*
to order	*āgyā dēnā*
to paint (to colour)	*rangnā, rang karnā*
to paint a picture	*chitra banānā*
to raise	*uṭhānā*
to read	*paṛhnā*
to receive	*pānā*

to recommend	*sifārish karnā*
to refuse	*manā karnā*
to regret	*afsōs karnā*
to reject	*asvikār karnā*
to remember	*yād karnā*
to rest	*ārām karnā*
to retu'rn	*lauṭānā*
to return (int.)	*lautanā*
to ring (the bell)	*ghanṭi bajānā*
to ride	*savār hōnā*
to rinse	*dhōnā*
to roast	*bhūnanā*
to run	*dauṛnā*
to run away	*bhāg jānā*
to say	*kahnā*
to scold	*danṭnā*
to search	*ḍhundhanā, khòjnā*
to see	*dèkhnā*
to sell	*bēchnā*
to send	*bhèjnā*
to send for	*bulā bhèjnā*
to serve	*sèvā karnā*
to sew	*sinā*
to shake	*hilānā*
to shake (int.)	*hilnā*
to shake hands	*hāth milānā*
to shave	*dāṛhi banānā*
to shout	*chillānā*
to show	*dikhānā*
to sing	*gānā*
to sink	*ḍūbanā*
to sit	*baiṭhanā*

to sleep	*sōnā*
to (put to) sleep	*sulānā*
to smell	*sūnghnā*
to smile	*muskarānā*
to sneeze	*chhīnknā*
to sow	*bōnā*
to speak	*bōlnā*
to spit	*thūknā*
to stand	*kharā hōnā*
to stay	*thaharnā*
to steal	*churānā, chōrī karnā*
to stop	*ruknā*
to strike	*mārnā*
to strike (work)	*hartāl karnā*
to study	*parhnā*
to suspect	*shak karnā*
to swear	*kasam khānā*
to swear (abuse)	*gālī dēnā*
to swim	*ta'rnā*
to take	*lēnā*
to taste	*chakhnā*
to tear	*pharnā*
to tell	*batānā*
to think	*sōchanā*
to try	*kōshish karnā*
to thank	*dhanyavād dēnā*
to throw	*phēnknā*
to tighten	*kasnā*
to translate	*anuvād karnā*
to understand	*samajhnā*
to undress	*kapre utārnā*
to use	*istēmāl karnā, upayōg karnā*

to utter	*kahnā*
to walk	*chalnā*
to walk for pleasure	*sair karnā*
to want	*chahnā*
to wash	*dhonā*
to waste	*barbād karnā*
to water (the plants)	*pani dēnā*
to wear	*pahan-nā*
to weave	*bunanā*
to weep	*rōnā*
to weigh	*tōlnā*
to whistle	*siṭi bajānā*
to wish	*chāhnā*
to win	*jitanā*
to work	*kām karnā*
to write	*likhnā*
to yell	*chillānā*

Some other useful words and phrases

to finish (int.)	*khatam hōnā*
to finish (tr.)	*khatam karnā*
specially, particularly	*khās kar*
please excuse me	*kshamā kijiyē, māf kijiyē*
sorry, I am late	*afsōs hai, dēr hō gayi*
I am early	*maiñ jaldi ā gayā*
does not matter	*kōi bāt nahiñ*
please don't mind	*burā na māniyē*
please	*kripayā, kripā kar kē meharbāni sē*
to put on shoes	*jūtā pahnanā*
to celebrate	*khushi manānā, utsava manānā*

to congratulate	*badhā-ī dēnā*
	mubārakbād dēnā
congratulations	*badhā-ī, mubārakbād*
happy new year	*nayā sāl mubārak hō*
best wishes for the new year	*nayē varsh kī shubha kamanāēñ*
good wishes for birthday	*janmadin mubārak hō*
good wishes	*shubha kāmanāēñ*

Various uses of the word *tēz*

The fever is high.	*bukhār tēz hai*
The sun is strong.	*dhūp tēz hai*
The knife is sharp.	*chhurī tēz hai*
The boy is sharp. (int.)	*laṛkā tēz hai*
The light is strong.	*roshanī tēz hai*
The wind is strong.	*havā tēz hai*
He runs fast.	*vah tēz dauṛatā hai*
Take tea after taking the medicine.	*davā khākar chāe pījiyē*
Sleep after eating.	*khānā khākar sō jāiyē*
I shall go for a walk after dinner.	*maiñ khānā khākar ghūmane jāūngā*
After reading tell me how the book is.	*paṛh kar batāiyē yah kitāb kaisī hai*

Cooking term

to bake	*sēnkanā*
to boil	*ubālnā*
to chill	*ṭhanḍā karnā*
to chop	*chhoṭē tukṛē karnā*
to cut	*kāṭanā*
to cover	*ḍhakanā*

to dice	*tukṛē kātanā*
to fry	*talnā*
to grate	*kasnā*
to grind	*pisanā*
to freeze	*jamānā*
to mash	*masalnā*
to peel	*chhilnā*
to scrape	*khurachanā*
spices	*masālē*
to strain	*chhānanā*
to season	*taḍkā dēnā*
to warm up	*garam karnā*
to wash	*dhōnā*

"The Wallah"

Some foreigners living in India have adopted the word 'wallah' to mean a hawker. Actually the word spelt phonetically is *vālā*, and by itself it does not have any meaning, but when combined with other words it has a variety of meanings. For example, when combined with the name of a commodity it would mean the seller of that particular commodity, *e.g.*,

sabzivālā	vegetable vendor
phalvālā	fruit vendor
phūlvālā	flower vendor
kapṛēvālā	cloth vendor
bartanvālā	utensils vendor
akhbārvālā	newspaperman
dūdhvālā	milkman
khilaunēvālā	toy-seller
taxīvālā	taxi driver

But that is not all. *Vālā* may be combined with the name of a city or town to mean a person belonging to that place, *e.g.*, *Dillivālā*, *Bombayvālā*, and so on.

Vālā is also used to specify a certain thing. For example *kalvālā akhbār*, means yesterday's newspaper; *ūparvālā kamarā* means the room upstairs. The meaning would be the same if you said *kalkā akhbār* or *upār kā kamarā*, but *vālā* is idiomatic and a colloquial expression.

●●●

VERB

Infinitive		Present Indefinite	Present Continuous	Present Perfect
*जाना	I s*	(मैं) जाता हूं	जा रहा हूं	गया हू
jānā		*(maiñ) jātā hūñ*	*jā rahā hūñ*	*gayā hūñ*
	p**	(हम) जाते हैं	जा रहे है	गये हैं
		(ham) jātē haiñ	*jā rahē hāiñ*	*gayē hāiñ*
	II s	(तुम) जाते हो	जा रहे हो	गए हो
		(tūm) jātē hō	*jā rahē hō*	*gayē hō*
		(आप) जाते हैं	जा रहे हैं	गए है
		(āp) jatē hāiñ	*jā rahē hāiñ*	*gayē hāiñ*
	p.	(आप लोग) जाते हैं	जा रहे हैं	गए है
		jātē hāiñ	*jā rahē hāiñ*	*gayē hāiñ*
	III s	(वह) जाता है	जा रहा है	गया है
		(vah) jāta hai	*jā rahā hai*	*gayā hai*
		(वे) जाते हैं	जा रहे हैं	गए हैं
		(ve) jatē haiñ	*jā rahē hāiñ*	*gayē hāiñ*
आना	I s	मैं आता हूं	आ रहा हूं	आया हूं
		(maiñ) ātā hūñ	*ā rahā hūñ*	*āyā hūñ*
	p	(हम) आते हैं	आ रहे हैं	आए हैं
		(ham) ātē hāiñ	*ā rahē hāiñ*	*ayē hāiñ*
	II s	(तुम) आते हो	आ रहे हो	तुम आये हो
		(tūm) ātē hō	*ārahē hō*	*tum āyē hō*
		(आप) आते हैं	आप आ रहे हैं	आप आये हैं
		(āp) ātē hāiñ	*ā rahē hāiñ*	*āp āyē hāiñ*
	III s	(वह) आता है	आ रहा है	आया है
		(voh) ātā hai	*ā rahā hai*	*āyā hai*
	p	(वे) आते हैं	आ रहे हैं	आए हैं
		(ve) ātē hāiñ	*ā rahē hāiñ*	*āyē hāiñ*

---

*s : singular, **p : plural

CHART

Past Indefinite	Past Continuous	Past Perfect	Future
जाता था	जा रहा था	गया था	जाऊंगा
jātā thā	*jā rahā thā*	*gayā thā*	*jāūñgā*
जाते थे	जा रहे थे	गये थे	जाएंगे
jātē thē	*jā rahē thē*	*gayē thē*	*jāeñge*
जाते थे	जा रहे थे	गये थे	जाओगे
jātē thē	*jā rahē thē*	*gayē thē*	*jāōge*
आते थे	जा रहे थे	गये थे	जाएंगे
jātē thē	*jā rahē thē*	*gayē thē*	*jāeñge*
जाते थे	जा रहे थे	गये थे	जाएंगे
jātē thē	*jā rahē thē*	*gayē thē*	*jāeñge*
जाता था	जा रहा था	गया था	जाएगा
jātā thā	*jā rahā thā*	*gayā thā*	*jāegā*
जाते थे	जा रहे थे	गये थे	जाएंगे
jatē thē	*jā rahē thē*	*gayē thē*	*jāeñge*
आता था	आ रहा था	आया था	आऊंगा
ātā thā	*ā rahā thā*	*āyā thā*	*āūñgā*
आते थे	आ रहे थे	आए थे	आएंगे
ātē thē	*ā rahē thē*	*āyē thē*	*āeñge*
तुम आते थे	तुम आ रहे थे	तुम आए थे	तुम आओगे
tum ātē thē	*tum ā rahē thē*	*tum āyē thē*	*tum āōge*
आप आते थे	आप आ रहे थे	आप आए थे	आप आएंगे
āp ātē thē	*āp ā rahē thē*	*āp āyē thē*	*āp āeñge*
आता था	आ रहा था	आया था	आएंगे
ātā thā	*ā rahā thā*	*āyā thā*	*āyēñge*
आते थे	आ रहे थे	आए थे	आएंगे
atē thē	*ā rahē thē*	*āyē thē*	*āyeñge*